AMY-JILL LEVINE

LIGHT *of* *the* WORLD

A BEGINNER'S GUIDE to ADVENT

Abingdon Press
Nashville

LIGHT OF THE WORLD
A Beginner's Guide to Advent

Copyright © 2019 Amy-Jill Levine
All rights reserved.

Library of Congress Catalog Control Number has been requested.

978-1-5018-8435-1

19 20 21 22 23 24 25 26 27 28 — 10 9 8 7 6 5 4 3 2
MANUFACTURED IN THE UNITED STATES OF AMERICA

Once again, to the churches, synods, presbyteries, dioceses,

and other Christian groups that have welcomed me,

in gratitude for your hospitality.

CONTENTS

Introduction 9

1. The Meaning of Memory 21

2. The Promise of Potential 53

3. The Journey to Joy 81

4. The Gifts of the Gentiles 111

Note 141

INTRODUCTION

"You are the light of the world. . . . Let your light shine before people, so they can see the good things you do and praise your Father who is in heaven."

Matthew 5:14, 16

Jesus spoke to the people again, saying, "I am the light of the world. Whoever follows me won't walk in darkness but will have the light of life."

John 8:12

I love Christmas. When I was a child, I sang Christmas carols in the public schools in North Dartmouth, Massachusetts, and to this day, in the car, or in the shower, or sometimes in the hallways of Vanderbilt Divinity School, I'll find myself humming "pa rum pa pum pum" or "fa la la la la." I did on occasion get the lyrics wrong: "Later on, we'll perspire, as we sit, by the fire" is comprehensible, but not quite right. My mother told me that I used to cry when I heard "Rudolph, the Red-Nosed Reindeer"; that the other reindeer would not play with him remains distressing to me.

When I was very little, I thought of Christmas as about tinsel and toys, candy canes and poinsettia plants. Seeing decorated trees inside people's homes, I'd think to myself, "Christians live here."

Houses that had lights on the outside indicated that the people inside were "really Christian." Somehow I got the impression that all these decorations were designed to make Jewish people happy. They certainly made me happy. They still do.

I also knew Christmas had something to do with a baby lying on straw and a pretty lady with a veil; there were some men in fancy bathrobes and crowns and other men in plain bathrobes with towels on their heads, and there was a donkey. But the story itself remained a mystery to me. I learned a little from the 1965 *A Charlie Brown Christmas*, in which Linus reads the story of the shepherds and the angels from Luke 2:8-14. The ending, from the King James Version, is the familiar (but not necessarily correct) translation from the Greek, "Glory to God in the highest, and on earth peace, good will toward men" (2:14). I liked the idea, but I did wonder what "peace on earth" had to do with Santa Claus, elves, or that donkey.

I still love Christmas, but now I appreciate not only the decorated tree but also the fruits the good trees bear. There is more beauty to Advent than Christmas music and artistic depictions of Madonna and Child. There is more value to the joy the season brings and the hopes it raises when we recognize the fascinating, rich, and provocative aspects of the stories of Jesus' birth.

Knowing the historical context of Linus's citation matters, as does recognizing how references to angels and shepherds in Luke 2:8-14 would have been heard two thousand years ago. How much more profound does the text read when we discover that, beneath the expression "good tidings of great joy," is the word for *Gospel*, *euangelion*, literally, "good news." The import of the text is enhanced when we see how mentions of the "city of David" and of King David himself are essential to the good news and when we see how divine rule and earthly peace are connected.

The more I read the Nativity stories in Matthew and Luke, the more drawn in I am; each sentence, each word, shimmers with significance—with allusions to Jewish texts and Roman history, with connections to other words and stories in the Gospels, and with multiple meanings for the present, about birth and death, youth and aging, taxation and immigration, revelation and hope—for any reader who opens the book. Each time I read these texts, I see something new; therefore, each time I read the texts, they still speak to me.

Knowing the history also helps us realize that Christmas is so much more than a children's holiday. I know a number of people who concluded that "Santa isn't real" and then leapt to the conclusion that the Christmas stories—of angelic appearances and prescient dreams, miraculous conceptions and stars that function like a GPS—are superstitious nonsense. Thus, they dismiss the first two chapters of Matthew and Luke; they relegate the Advent messages to the space next to the elf on the shelf (not to be confused with Hanukkah's "mensch on a bench") where the Gospel chapters gather dust alongside the little drummer boy, the manger in the snow globe, and "Olive, the other reindeer."

I've met far too many people, and in this case one person is too many, who have left the church because they could not "believe" the Christmas stories. Still others, noticing discrepancies in the narratives—Matthew has Magi, and Luke has shepherds; Matthew locates Joseph and Mary in their home in Bethlehem, and Luke has the birth in a stable; the genealogies of Joseph disagree, and so on—conclude that both accounts are untrustworthy.

The problem in each case is one of category confusion. Those who dismiss Matthew 1–2 and Luke 1–2 as mythological drivel have read the texts incorrectly. Matthew and Luke are not writing for children, and the stories are anything but childish. Nor are they writing newspaper reports striving for historical accuracy. These Gospels

seek to tell us, we readers then and now, about the connection of the good news of Jesus both to the story of Israel and to the gentile world, about the clash of imperial and heavenly values, about a world for which many of us hope but not enough have the chance to find. To express such important, such sublime, messages, they write to spark our imaginations, to get us to see otherwise.

Not all people are able to believe these stories as accounts of what actually happened. I am among them. While the Christmas stories are set in historical time, the reigns of Herod the Great and Augustus Caesar are designed less to "record what happened" than to set the scene: to explain to readers removed from that time and place what the birth of Jesus signifies. For people who believe the Gospel writers are recording "what exactly happened," this study will enhance that belief. For people who are inclined to dismiss the stories as inconsistent, or unbelievable, this study will show how inspirational, challenging, and profound they are. We should even celebrate the distinct stories Matthew and Luke offer, since the import of what they recount must be told from multiple perspectives. Something so momentous cannot be contained in a single version. Indeed, if I as an outsider can see such value in these texts, surely those who are within the Christianity communion can find even more.

Studying the Bible should focus not only on learning the *what* in terms of what the texts say but also on determining the *so what* in terms of how the story conveys the good news that Matthew and Luke, and countless others, found in the conception and birth of Jesus of Nazareth. That *so what* is found when we, each one of us, encounter the text for ourselves.

What keeps us from going off the deep end in our interpretations (no, the star of Bethlehem is not about a UFO; no, Gabriel is not a Martian) is the rest of the Bible plus the two-thousand-year tradition of interpretation. Reading the Bible begins with the immediate

encounter between the individual and the text; here we ask, "What does this text mean to me, at this moment, in this place?" But our reading should not stop here. We should also ask, "What has this text meant to others in my life, in my church, in history, in the world?" All our readings are necessarily partial: we will never see everything the text has to convey.

The Nativity accounts had to fulfill two functions: they had to enlighten, and they also had to entice, to draw us more deeply into the chapters that follow. The Evangelists were writing primarily to insiders who want to know more, as Luke 1:1-4 indicates. When we recognize the historical background and the literary art, we can see how brilliantly the Evangelists, in quite different ways, accomplished their goals.

One problem for many of us today is that we do not know what was familiar to the people who lived two thousand years ago, whether Jews who witnessed the last years of the reign of Herod the Great, or Jews and gentiles both, followers of Jesus, who first heard the Gospels of Matthew and Luke. As with any biblical text, if we get the history wrong, not only will we miss the allusions to other texts as well as events, but also we risk misunderstanding the Gospel messages. Bad history leads to bad theology.

Bad history also leads to bad science and to bad literary interpretation. For example, unless we answer such questions as "Who was Herod the Great?" "Who were the Magi?" and "How did people in the first-century Mediterranean world understand stars?" we can never understand Matthew 2. Unless we recognize how Matthew seeks to show Jesus as a new Moses, we will miss the import of the slaughter of Bethlehem's children. And unless we know the original context of Rachel's weeping for her children, we will not hear the voice of comfort beneath the lament.

Such historical study is not designed to call into question Christian doctrine. God forbid, or as Paul would say in Greek, *me genoito*, "no way." Biblical studies should not seek to undermine belief; it should function to enhance it.

This concern for enhancing belief may sound strange coming from me. I am not a Christian, although I have spent over half a century (yes, I'm *that* old) studying the New Testament and its interpretations over time and across the globe. In my teaching, whether in Nashville at Vanderbilt Divinity School or in the spring of 2019 in Rome, where I was the first Jew to teach a New Testament course at the Pontifical Biblical Institute, I seek to enrich the Gospel proclamation by helping my students see the history behind the text, the literary and aesthetic implications in the text, and the multiple ways the text can be interpreted to address the needs of the people who hold it sacred.

At the same time, I regard these Gospel stories as Jewish stories and so part of my own history. Matthew and Luke quote Jewish sources, draw on Jewish images, are set in the Jewish homeland, and describe a Jewish messiah. If we miss that context, we'll also miss much of the message. Worse, if we get the Jewish context wrong, we might find ourselves inventing or perpetuating anti-Jewish stereotypes. Gospel proclamation should never be an occasion for bigotry. It is also my hope that more Jews would read these Advent stories and so recognize that Christmas is more than tinsel, or that donkey. In fact, I find the more I study this material, the better Jew I become, because I become more informed about the Jewish history that is the Christmas story (okay, the ivy and mistletoe, reindeer and yule log, and tinsel and tree are not Jewish; then again, neither are they in the Gospels).

Along with Matthew's and Luke's numerous allusions to and explicit statements concerning Jews and Judaism is the connection

between Jewish and Christian tradition in popular culture. Just as Lent reminds me of the Jewish "Days of Awe," the time between the New Year (Rosh HaShanah) and the Day of Atonement (Yom Kippur)—the time of introspection when we Jews reflect on what we have done, what we should have done, and what we resolve to do; the time when we apologize to anyone we have hurt, by wrong action or by failing to act—so Christmas reminds me of Hanukkah, another winter festival (at least in the Northern Hemisphere). *Hanukkah* is the Hebrew word for "dedication," and it is mentioned in the Gospel of John, where Jesus visits the Temple: "The time came for the Festival of Dedication in Jerusalem. It was winter" (John 10:22).

When I was little, I believed not in Santa Claus (if my memory is correct, the Santa at the big department store in New Bedford was a fellow who attended our synagogue and spoke with a slight Yiddish accent) but in the Hanukkah Fairy who gave gifts to children, one each night for the eight-day holiday. I thought the Hanukkah Fairy was the sister of the Blue Fairy in Pinocchio, the fairy godmother who sang "Bibbidi-Bobbidi-Boo" in *Cinderella*, the Tooth Fairy, and Tinkerbell from *Peter Pan*. Then I learned that Hanukkah is about a fight for freedom of religion. The fascination continued as I told the story to my own children.

The same changes hold for the Christmas story: from a child's delight, to growing awareness of the literature and the context, to appreciation of the art and the music through a child's eyes and ears, and then back to the text. Its lessons are never ending, beautiful, and inspirational.

The chapters that follow take us through the four weeks of Advent. The first, "The Meaning of Memory," turns to Luke 1:5-25 and then 57-79, the story of Zechariah and Elizabeth.

The story transports us back to Abraham and Sarah, Isaac and Rebecca, and several other couples in Israel's Scriptures who suffered

from infertility. We'll see the humor—yes, laugh-out-loud humor—in Zechariah's encounter with the angel, and we'll see how family traditions can be modified, here with a woman's insistence. This opening story, which will make us smile with joy, is the perfect entry to the Christmas season, where what is old becomes new again and where delight, at least for a moment, replaces despair.

Chapter 2, "The Promise of Potential," picks up with Gabriel's announcement to the virgin engaged to Joseph, "Rejoice, favored one," and Mary's appropriate confusion; it's not every day that angels appear. Mary hears the startling news of her forthcoming pregnancy, agrees to the angel's words, and then hurries to the Judean highlands to confirm the angel's notice of Elizabeth's pregnancy.

It is to Elizabeth that Mary sings the song traditionally called the Magnificat, the song that begins, "With all my heart I glorify the Lord!" (Luke 1:46). Mary sings not only of divine glory; she sings also of ancient promises of social revolution. She sings the songs of Miriam and Deborah and Hannah, but in a new key for a new time.

From Mary's visit with Elizabeth we see not only the importance of solidarity, across the generations, between women, but also the importance of the human body, which provides its own signs of new beginnings. We see how revolutionary ideas can be given voice not just in the university or the town hall, but in the quiet hill country homes; not just by soldiers with arms or politicians with pens, but by mothers with song.

Finally, we see in Mary a model for ecumenical and interfaith relations. Mary sings that "everyone will consider me highly favored" (Luke 1:48). She is honored especially in Roman Catholicism, Eastern Orthodoxy, and even in Islam. Yet she is part of the Protestant Bible as well, and she is a Jewish woman. Perhaps Mary, understood differently and yet shared across faiths, will become a bridge among us.

In chapter 3, "The Journey to Joy," we accompany Joseph and Mary from Nazareth in Galilee to Bethlehem in Judea, where Jesus will be born in a stable, because, as the familiar saying goes, "there was no room at the inn." Here we also see how the "manger" anticipates Jesus' Last Supper; it is much more than just a bed of straw.

In chapter 3 we also meet Simeon and Anna, two elderly Jews in the Jerusalem Temple. Simeon and Anna, like Zechariah and Elizabeth, represent fidelity to the ancient traditions. We can see them handing on to the next generation, to Mary and Joseph and to the child, the trust that they will guard the stories and practices of the Jewish people.

The presentation of Jesus in the Temple strikes another important chord: the importance of what we today would call "institutional religion." In these days when "I'm spiritual but not religious" is often heard, and when churches are closing because of dwindling membership and deferred maintenance, the presentation shows us the importance of the organized religious community. Simeon and Anna are not participating in a "make it up as you go along" system. They are part of a community, a tradition, and a legacy.

Chapter 4 turns from Israel to "The Gifts of the Gentiles." We first spot gentiles in the New Testament's opening verse, Matthew 1:1: "A record of the ancestors of Jesus Christ, son of David, the son of Abraham." Abraham, recognized as the first Jew as well as the first to be "justified by faith" (so Romans 4), begins his life as a pagan. Then things change. Matthew's genealogy records the names of several gentiles who join Abraham's descendants: Tamar, Rahab, Ruth, and then perhaps Bathsheba, the wife of Uriah (we do know that Uriah himself was a gentile, a Hittite), and what stories they have to tell.

Even more, what might be called the "obstetrical irregularities" of their lives anticipate Jesus' virginal conception. According to Matthew, Joseph, "son of Jacob," is a true descendant of that first "Joseph son of Jacob," who according to Genesis, dreamed dreams and took his family to Egypt. Our Joseph dreams of an angel who tells him not

to divorce his pregnant fiancée, for Mary's pregnancy fulfills Isaiah's prediction of a virgin conceiving.

Finally, we'll visit with the Magi, who are neither kings nor necessarily just three nor, according to Matthew, wise. We'll learn why the star of Bethlehem is not an actual star, how to assess the role of Herod, whom Matthew calls "king of the Jews," and what texts accompany the tragic "Slaughter of the Innocents."

We end with the return of Mary, Joseph, and Jesus to Nazareth. Like that mustard seed, on the outskirts of the empire, in a small Galilean village, something small is about to become something marvelous, beyond expectations.

Chapter 1

THE MEANING OF MEMORY

Chapter 1

THE MEANING OF MEMORY

*During the rule of King Herod of Judea there was a priest
named Zechariah who belonged to the priestly division of
Abijah. His wife Elizabeth was a descendant of Aaron.
They were both righteous before God, blameless in their
observance of all the Lord's commandments and regulations.
They had no children because Elizabeth was unable to
become pregnant and they both were very old. One day
Zechariah was serving as a priest before God because his
priestly division was on duty. Following the customs of
priestly service, he was chosen by lottery to go into the Lord's
sanctuary and burn incense. All the people who gathered
to worship were praying outside during this hour of incense
offering. An angel from the Lord appeared to him, standing
to the right of the altar of incense. When Zechariah saw the
angel, he was startled and overcome with fear.*

*The angel said, "Don't be afraid, Zechariah. Your prayers
have been heard. Your wife Elizabeth will give birth to your
son and you must name him John. He will be a joy and
delight to you, and many people will rejoice at his birth, for
he will be great in the Lord's eyes. He must not drink wine*

and liquor. He will be filled with the Holy Spirit even before his birth. He will bring many Israelites back to the Lord their God. He will go forth before the Lord, equipped with the spirit and power of Elijah. He will turn the hearts of fathers back to their children, and he will turn the disobedient to righteous patterns of thinking. He will make ready a people prepared for the Lord."

Zechariah said to the angel, "How can I be sure of this? My wife and I are very old."

The angel replied, "I am Gabriel. I stand in God's presence. I was sent to speak to you and to bring this good news to you. Know this: What I have spoken will come true at the proper time. But because you didn't believe, you will remain silent, unable to speak until the day when these things happen."

Meanwhile, the people were waiting for Zechariah, and they wondered why he was in the sanctuary for such a long time. When he came out, he was unable to speak to them. They realized he had seen a vision in the temple, for he gestured to them and couldn't speak. When he completed the days of his priestly service, he returned home. Afterward, his wife Elizabeth became pregnant. She kept to herself for five months, saying, "This is the Lord's doing. He has shown his favor to me by removing my disgrace among other people." . . .

When the time came for Elizabeth to have her child, she gave birth to a boy. Her neighbors and relatives celebrated with her because they had heard that the Lord had shown her great mercy. On the eighth day, it came time to circumcise the child. They wanted to name him Zechariah because that was his father's name. But his mother replied, "No, his name will be John."

They said to her, "None of your relatives have that name."
Then they began gesturing to his father to see what he
wanted to call him.

After asking for a tablet, he surprised everyone by writing,
"His name is John." At that moment, Zechariah was able to
speak again, and he began praising God.

All their neighbors were filled with awe, and everyone
throughout the Judean highlands talked about what had
happened. All who heard about this considered it carefully.
They said, "What then will this child be?" Indeed, the Lord's
power was with him.

John's father Zechariah was filled with the Holy Spirit and
prophesied,

> "Bless the Lord God of Israel
>> because he has come to help and has delivered his
>> people.
> He has raised up a mighty savior for us in his servant
> David's house,
>> just as he said through the mouths of his holy
>> prophets long ago.
> He has brought salvation from our enemies
>> and from the power of all those who hate us.
> He has shown the mercy promised to our ancestors,
>> and remembered his holy covenant,
>>> the solemn pledge he made to our ancestor
>>> Abraham.
> He has granted that we would be rescued
>> from the power of our enemies
>> so that we could serve him without fear,
>>> in holiness and righteousness in God's eyes,
>>> for as long as we live.

You, child, will be called a prophet of the Most High,
    for you will go before the Lord to prepare his way.
You will tell his people how to be saved
    through the forgiveness of their sins.
Because of our God's deep compassion,
    the dawn from heaven will break upon us,
    to give light to those who are sitting in darkness
    and in the shadow of death,
      to guide us on the path of peace."
Luke 1:5-25, 57-79

Where and when we were born, the place and the time, are part of our identity; the details are recorded in our passports, and they will be mentioned in our obituaries. Yet we are an increasingly mobile society, one focused on the present and the future. Many of my students cannot name the president in office the year they were born, they have no clue about the Vietnam War, and mentions of the "summer of '67" evoke the response, "67 what?" And in the focus on youth, growth, and the future, many churches take for granted their congregation's older members. To ignore them is to ignore our history and heritage.

Knowing the where and when of Jesus is essential for understanding him. The Temple in Jerusalem, Bethlehem in Judea, Nazareth in Galilee, and Egypt where the family finds shelter—are more than just locations, and the reigns of Herod the King and Augustus Caesar more than dates. When the Evangelists mention a date and a place, they are telling us to pay attention, for time and space hold a surfeit of meaning. And when Luke chooses to begin this magnificent story not with Mary and Joseph but with Elizabeth and Zechariah, we pay attention as well, since this couple represents the older generation, our connection to the past, our communal memory.

This is no dry history lesson of names and dates, and Luke is nothing like the ivy-covered professor who can only state facts. Luke is a storyteller, and what a story this is. This elderly, and so-far infertile, couple will join Abraham and Sarah, and many others, in learning that they will have a child. Luke's recounting of the angel's conversation with the soon-to-be-dumbstruck Zechariah brilliantly weds the conventional to the comic. In recounting the story of John's birth and naming, Luke again combines miracle and memory. More than just Elizabeth, Zechariah, and their friends and relatives will rejoice at this birth, for the story should make all but the most somber of readers laugh with joy.

In the Days of King Herod

Following a four-verse prologue in which Luke, in elegant Greek, lists his purposes for writing, the narrative proper begins: "During the rule of King Herod of Judea" (Luke 1:5). This is not an auspicious start. Readers familiar with Matthew's Gospel know of a King Herod who ordered the massacre of the children in Bethlehem in the attempt to kill the baby Jesus, a rival king. While it is not clear whether this slaughter actually took place, it is not unthinkable given Herod's other outrages: he killed his own sons, whom he suspected of plotting against him; he killed his wife Mariamne, the Hasmonean princess, as well as her brother and her mother. According to the first-century Jewish historian Josephus, Herod realized that the people he ruled hated him, whether for his taxes, for his replacing the High Priest in the Temple, for sponsoring pagan cities, or for killing his family members—the list goes on. Therefore, as he was dying, he ordered that "the whole nation should be put into mourning, and indeed made desolate of their dearest kindred, when he gave order that one out of every family should be slain" (*Antiquities* 17.181). The orders were not carried out, but the memory remained.

People in Luke's original audience also would have heard of Herod. He was the one who began the reconstruction of the Jerusalem Temple, he built the port of Caesarea Maritima, and he constructed numerous fortresses including one on Masada. His building projects still stand as testimony to his reign; to see the buildings without knowing the history behind them is insufficient. Any story set in the reign of King Herod is a story of political intrigue and of threats to life. This is the context, Luke tells us, of the conception and birth of John the Baptizer, who will die by the order of Herod Antipas, the son of Herod the Great.

Luke tells us more, for the opening verses anticipate another king, and another birth. Herod is a major political player, but he has his overlords. After siding with Marc Antony and Cleopatra, he shifted his loyalty to Caesar Augustus and so managed to keep in Rome's good graces. It will be this same Caesar who, according to Luke, ordered the census that brought Joseph and Mary to Bethlehem. Jesus' birth is set "in those days [when] Caesar Augustus declared that everyone throughout the empire should be enrolled in tax lists" (Luke 2:1). His birth has universal import.

Zechariah and Elizabeth

Herod is not the only person Luke introduces in chapter 1 verse 5. The verse in full reads, "During the rule of King Herod of Judea there was a priest named Zechariah who belonged to the priestly division of Abijah. His wife Elizabeth was a descendant of Aaron."

In antiquity family makes a difference. That's why both Matthew and Luke provide genealogies placing Jesus in the line of Abraham, Judah, and King David. At the same time, the biblical tradition insists that an illustrious background is not prerequisite for fulfilling divine will or for making our own mark on history. Luke signals this point by another contrast: we learn of Elizabeth's priestly connections, but as

we'll see, Mary's background, save for her connection to Elizabeth, goes unremarked. What is important in the Bible is not our pedigree or our ancestry, but our action.

Herod holds the throne, but Zechariah and Elizabeth are the focus of our attention. An immediate contrast appears: king versus priest, foreign interloper versus loyal children of Israel. To reinforce this focus on Zechariah and Elizabeth, and even signal a rejection of Herod's Roman connections, Luke changes style. The first four verses are ornate, formal, classical Roman rhetoric. But with verse 5, Luke shifts to the language of the Septuagint, the Greek translation of what will become the Old Testament.

The shift in the Greek is palpable, like going from modern English to Shakespearean language. With this shift, Luke takes us to the past, the world of early Jewish history. Luke thus insists: to understand Jesus requires understanding Jewish history and Jewish texts. More, Luke is telling gentile converts: this history of Israel is now part of your history as well. It is part of your story. Read, remember, and rejoice.

The name *Zechariah* comes from the Hebrew root *z-k-r*, which means "remember"; the "yah" at the end is the marker for YHWH, so the name means "God remembers." Memory is a trait of the biblical God. Already following the Flood, God promises Noah and so all humanity, "I will remember the covenant between me and you and every living being among all the creatures. Floodwaters will never again destroy all creatures" (Genesis 9:15).

The Jewish tradition even records Psalms and other prayers in which we remind God to remember us. For example, Psalm 119:49 reads, "Remember your promise to your servant, / for which you made me wait." When we feel the absence of the divine, when we think there is no reason to hope, we call out to God to remember, because we remember. We can do so because we know that the covenant

is permanent. It is this sense of a loving, permanent covenant that underlies the rawness and honesty of Jesus' cry from the cross in Matthew (27:46) and Mark (15:34), "My God, my God, why have you left me?" The cry is the first line of Psalm 22, and we remember that it ends with redemption: "Every part of the earth / will remember and come back to the LORD; / every family among all the nations will worship you" (Psalm 22:27).

God also commands us to remember. Numbers 15:39 mandates, "This will be your fringe. You will see it and remember all the LORD's commands and do them. Then you won't go exploring the lusts of your own heart or your eyes." These are the fringes Jesus wears, and that the woman with the hemorrhage reaches out to touch (see Luke 8:44). Deuteronomy uses the refrain, "Remember that you were a slave in Egypt" (5:15 and elsewhere); that experience grounds Israel's ethics.

In Judaism, *yizkor* (from the same root) is the service, held four times a year, in which we Jews recall our family members, friends, and other members of our community, especially the martyrs, from the six million killed in the Shoah to more recent shootings in synagogues in Pittsburgh and Poway. The service is not simply one of commemoration; we also pledge to honor that memory by giving to charity and doing works of righteousness. In that way, the name of the deceased can be a blessing.

Ephesians 2:12 takes up the refrain: "At that time you were without Christ. You were aliens rather than citizens of Israel, and strangers to the covenants of God's promise. In this world you had no hope and no God." We cannot know fully who we are, unless we know our origins. With new experiences, we will then reassess those origins. That is the message Luke gives: in light of these new stories, we find new meaning in the past.

When we feel the absence of the divine, when we think there is no reason to hope, we call out to God to remember, because we remember. We can do so because we know that the covenant is permanent.

Elizabeth's name likely derives from the Hebrew *Eli*, meaning "my God," the beginning of Jesus' cry from the cross ("My God, my God"). The second part comes from *sheva*, which is an oath. Thus, her name indicates that God keeps promises. That means that God remembers. An earlier Elisheba is the wife of Aaron, the first Israelite priest (Exodus 6:23).

Zechariah and Elizabeth are from priestly families, descended from Aaron. Priesthood in Judaism is not a vocation but a matter of paternal descent. If your father is a priest, you are a priest. If your father is a Levite, a type of subordinate priest descended from Aaron's ancestor Levi, the third son of Jacob and Leah, then you are a Levite. To this day, Jews know who the priests and Levites are. One clue, although it is not always reliable, is one's name. The names *Cohen*, *Kane*, and *Kaplan* often indicate priestly descent, since the Hebrew word for "priest" is *cohen*. *Levine*, *Levy*, *Levison*, and so on may indicate levitical (from *Levi*) descent. Although the Jerusalem Temple was destroyed, certain practices in Judaism related to priests and Levites remain. For example, in many synagogues, priests and Levites have the honor of being called, respectively, first and second to say the blessing before and after the Torah reading on Shabbat (Sabbath/Saturday) morning.

With Elizabeth, Luke introduces another theme: the importance of women in the Gospel. The CEB translation, "descendant of Aaron," misses the nuance of the Greek, which literally says she is from the "daughters of Aaron." *Daughter* echoes through Luke's Gospel: Anna the "daughter of Phanuel," the prophet who greets the baby Jesus in the Temple, the ruler's "daughter" whom Jesus raises from the dead, the "daughter" whose hemorrhages Jesus dries up, the "daughter of Abraham" who receives her healing in the synagogue, and the "daughters of Jerusalem" who weep for Jesus. Along with the

births of sons, John and Jesus, there are also daughters, who are to be remembered and celebrated.

With Zechariah and Elizabeth, there is much to celebrate, since "they were both righteous before God, blameless in their observance of all the Lord's commandments and regulations" (Luke 1:6). The Greek for "righteous" is *dikaios*, another word that appears throughout the Gospel. Among several examples: Gabriel predicts that John will turn "the disobedient to the wisdom of the righteous" (Luke 1:17 NIV); Simeon, who with Anna sees Jesus in the Temple, was "righteous and devout" (Luke 2:25); the centurion at the cross, witnessing Jesus die, proclaims him *dikaios*. "Righteousness" for Luke does not mean having the correct theology. Righteousness means behaving in a way marked by justice.

A number of my Christian students, having heard that there are 613 laws, regard following the commandments (Hebrew: *mitzvot*; the terms *bar mitzvah* and *bat mitzvah* literally mean, respectively, "son or daughter of commandment") as a burden and then give thanks that they are not "under the Law." Traditionally, there are 613 laws in the Torah, and Judaism through the centuries has added more, as times and places change. But they are hardly burdensome. There are more laws in every U.S. state than there are in the Jewish legal corpus. Nor are they impossible to follow. Paul agrees when he gives his autobiographical credentials, "with respect to righteousness under the Law, I'm blameless" (Philippians 3:6b).

For Elizabeth and Zechariah, for Paul, and for their fellow Jews, following the *mitzvot* is a blessing. We might think of these commandments as a template for multiculturalism. Within the Roman imperial context of Jesus and Paul, the Torah allowed Jews proudly to proclaim their own distinct identity through honoring the Sabbath and various feasts and fasts, to going on pilgrimage to the

Jerusalem Temple, to paying attention to what they wear and what they eat. Such things we remember when we look at those fringes, when we recall our history, when we celebrate our identities and our past.

The Jerusalem Temple

Although righteous, Zechariah and Elizabeth were childless, and, since Elizabeth had gone through menopause (Luke phrases this more discreetly), there was little hope for a pregnancy (Luke 1:7). Luke makes clear that her infertility is not the result of sin; the rest of the Bible makes the same point. The matriarchs Sarah, Rebecca, and Rachel all struggled with infertility, as did Mrs. Manoah, the mother of the judge Samson, Hannah the mother of the prophet Samuel, and the "great woman of Shunem" who was Elisha's patron. According to the Bible, it is God who opens and closes wombs; prospective parents are not to be blamed for their childless state. Rather, by noting the problem of infertility, the Bible allows readers to address it.

When the Bible mentions righteous couples suffering from infertility, a conception is not far behind. We can also anticipate that one or both of the parents will encounter a messenger—often an angel, sometimes a priest or prophet—to predict that conception. Remember, Luke advises, you have seen this story before. You are about to hear it again, but with a new couple, at a new time, with a new message.

The setting for this anticipated annunciation is in the Temple. Zechariah is not a high priest like Caiaphas, based in Jerusalem; he is an ordinary village priest, like the priest in Jesus' parable of the good Samaritan. There were far too many priests in Israel for all to serve in the Temple (unlike the clergy shortage that some churches face), so they had to work out a system for all the priests to serve.

Zechariah was chosen by lot to perform the incense offering (1:9). Casting lots, not uncommon in biblical texts, is a fair way of dividing property or duties. Proverbs 18:18 states, "Casting the lot puts an end to disputes / and decides between powerful contenders" (NRSV). Luke will repeat this motif in 23:34 (the soldiers cast lots for Jesus' clothing) and Acts 1:26 (to determine the replacement for Judas Iscariot). In such matters, whether casting lots in the Bible or a coin toss to see which team goes first, we can choose to see divine providence, or not.

In performing the incense offering, Zechariah will not be swinging a censer of the sort that for me evokes Tallulah Bankhead's comment to Cardinal Cody, "Darling, I love your dress but your purse is on fire." He places the incense on the incense altar (see Exodus 30). The Jewish tradition has always been one of sensory delights: sights and sounds, scents and tastes, attention to the body. Worship not only is spiritually uplifting and beneficial for community relations but also should be aesthetically pleasing: it gives us, when it can, the gift of beauty, something often needed in a world marked by bullets, poverty, and disease.

Let's savor the scene. The magnificent building, priests and the worshipers, Jews and pagans, from Europe and Asia and North Africa, sounds of Levites singing and children laughing, the smells of incense, and animals, even the tastes of the meat of the sacrifices. Worship at its best is something that engages not just the mind but the body.

It is the time of the afternoon incense offering, and "all the people who gathered to worship were praying outside during this hour of incense offering" (Luke 1:10). Prayer, a motif Luke repeats, begins here. Some perhaps were praying, as Zechariah and Elizabeth had, for children; others for health or healing; still others for the well-being of the people, or for thanksgiving, or, perhaps, for Herod to

take a long vacation. Or perhaps some were praying for the Messiah to bring about the kingdom of heaven.

The Angel's Good News

We know, since we've been told of the couple's childlessness, that an annunciation is near. We are not disappointed. The angel appears. In later biblical texts, angels appear with some frequency, sometimes in disguise, sometimes to interpret visions (as in the Book of Daniel), and sometimes to make announcements. The Epistle to the Hebrews (13:2) warns, "Don't neglect to open up your homes to guests, because by doing this some have been hosts to angels without knowing it." The verse alludes to Genesis 18, the story of how Abraham and Sarah, our first righteous but infertile couple, heard that they would have a child.

Seeing the angel, Zechariah is, not surprisingly, terrified (Luke 1:12 NRSV). "Terrified" or "afraid" is *tarasso*, with the connotation of being shaken up. The same term appears in Matthew's Gospel (2:3) to describe King Herod's reaction to the report of a newborn King of the Jews. The only other time the verb appears in Luke's Gospel is in the story of the two on the road to Emmaus, when Jesus asks them: "Why are you startled? Why are doubts arising in your hearts?" (24:38). To use the colloquialism, he's about to rock their world.

This sense of being shaken up is Advent good news. Christmas should be more than putting up the tree and wrapping the presents. It should give birth to something that shakes up the routine, something that gets us to see the world otherwise. That shaking up is what it means to follow Jesus. To love one's enemies is scary; to take up one's cross is terrifying. Yet at the same time, Luke reminds us, there is a legacy that carries us forward and a promise that God will remember the covenant and bring about eternal justice.

The angel immediately reassures the terrified priest: "Your prayers have been heard." The prayer, although unstated, was for a child: "Your wife Elizabeth will give birth to your son" (1:13a). Personal prayer is not selfish but honest; we should share our concerns with God. The famous Jewish teacher and slightly older contemporary of Jesus, Hillel, is quoted in the Mishnah, "If I am not for myself, who is for me? And when I am for myself, what am I? And if not now, when?" (*Avot* 1.14). We must, if the need arises, pray for ourselves. Jesus tells a parable about a tax collector who prays, "God, show mercy to me, a sinner" (Luke 18:13). We pray for ourselves, but we cannot be concerned only for ourselves.

Luke will continue the motif of prayer: Jesus prays, the disciples ask Jesus to teach them to pray as John taught his disciples, and so on. But Luke also humorously tweaks those who pray but do not act. Acts 12, which begins with a reference to "King Herod"—here Herod Agrippa I who reigned in the forties—describes how after killing James the brother of John, Herod imprisoned Peter. An angel breaks Peter out, and Peter makes his way to the home of Mary the mother of John Mark, where Jesus' followers have gathered. The congregation is upstairs praying, quite likely for Peter's release. Peter knocks at the gate. The Greek text reports that a slave (a "maid" in the NRSV [Acts 12:13]) named Rhoda reports to the assembled that Peter is at the gate. But they tell her, "'You've lost your mind!'. . . She stuck by her story with such determination that they began to say, 'It must be his guardian angel'" (Acts 12:15).

Peter continues to knock. When they finally open the gate, Peter instructs them to convey a message to James and then walks away. No use praying with this group. Luke gently criticizes people who pray, and pray, but who fail to open the gate, or to see the need at their doorstep.

Even without the angelic announcement, there are expectations placed especially on only children, or children born to comparatively older parents. It is their role to carry the family name; it is their responsibility to care for their parents.

The angel continues this good news by announcing to Zechariah, "You must name him John" (Luke 1:13b). John was a common name at the time, including John the brother of James and John the author of the Book of Revelation. The Hebrew *Yochanan* means "God [Yo, as in YHWH] is gracious."

That "many people will rejoice at his birth" (1:14) indicates more than sharing Zechariah and Elizabeth's happiness that their prayers have been answered. The people, as we shall see, expect something special from this child. Even without the angelic announcement, there are expectations placed especially on only children, or children born to comparatively older parents. It is their role to carry the family name; it is their responsibility to care for their parents.

Or, perhaps I am projecting. My mother, who struggled with infertility and a number of miscarriages, was forty-four when I was born, and I am an only child. Then again, no angel appeared to her, as far as I am aware.

John will be one of many who, in Luke-Acts, are filled with the Holy Spirit. The Spirit drives the plot of Luke-Acts. It appears next in Gabriel's annunciation to Mary, and then Elizabeth's recognition that the "mother of [her] Lord" has come to her (Luke 1:43). The Spirit is literally pregnant with meaning, bringing new life. That metaphor works better in Hebrew, where the Spirit is *ruach*, a feminine noun.

The Hebrew comes into Greek as *pneuma*, a term that like the Hebrew can also mean "wind" or "breath" (as in "pneumonia" or "pneumatic"). It inspires; it animates; it can literally knock us over. The Greek noun *pneuma* is, unlike the Hebrew, neuter (as opposed to masculine or feminine). This shift in genders is appropriate for the Spirit, which as the Gospel of John (3:8) puts it, "blows wherever it wishes."

In John's case, the Spirit marks him as a new Elijah: Gabriel announces, "He will bring many Israelites back to the Lord their God.

He will go forth before the Lord, equipped with the spirit and power of Elijah. He will turn the hearts of fathers back to their children, and he will turn the disobedient to righteous patterns of thinking. He will make ready a people prepared for the Lord" (Luke 1:16-17). The point is not that everyone had gotten off track, as Zechariah and Elizabeth and the people outside the Temple demonstrate. The point is preparation for the messianic age. Christian readers will take turning to "the Lord their God" as a reference to Jesus, called "Lord" (Greek: *kyrios*).

Two of many notices in the angel's words stand out: the first is the reference to Elijah and the second is the term *turn*. Here again, knowledge of the Jewish context enriches our understanding.

The prophet Malachi had predicted that Elijah would return from the heavens (he was transported up with a fiery chariot, hence, "swing low, sweet chariot"); Elijah, the forerunner of the "great and terrifying day of the LORD," will "*turn* the hearts of the parents to the children and the hearts of the children to their parents" (Malachi 4:5-6, italics added). The prediction concerns the messianic age, the end of time as we know it.

Luke rereads the prophecy to speak of the coming of the Messiah; the messianic age, with its resurrection of the dead, final judgment, and establishment of peace, health, and security, will have to wait until Jesus' return.

Such rereadings are to be expected in biblical interpretation. In light of present events, we understand the past differently. In light of Jesus, his followers come to understand the Scriptures of Israel differently. And in light of our own experiences, we will, if we look closely, always see new things in, and hear new messages from, ancient stories. We remember, but our memories are always being reshaped. We remember the past, but we are not to be prisoners of it. New understandings of past events inevitably arise.

Elijah, and John, will help in turning the people. Turning requires action. It is not simply an internal sense of contrition; it is taking action to restore correct relationships. That concern returns us to memory. To "turn" means to look back and see where we got off track. It means asking, "What should I have done that I did not do? What did I do that I should not have done? How do I get on the right road and then walk forward?"

For Malachi, turning mean parents saying to their children, "I'm sorry I did not spend more time with you when you were younger," or "I'm sorry I projected onto you my own concerns." It means being like the father of the prodigal son and his prudent older brother and making sure that both feel loved and valued. It means adult children saying to their parents, "I'm sorry I became impatient with you; I'm sorry I did not call or visit," and then making sure that occasions requiring apologies surface less often.

When people turn to the right path, when the disobedient turn to the wisdom of the righteous (so Luke 1:17), then they are "a people prepared for the Lord." But this preparation always comes with a cost. We can imagine the later conversations John would have with his parents, or Jesus with Mary and Joseph. What happens when the child decides to risk life for justice? What do we, the parents, say?

Zechariah's Doubt

Instead of asking about the Spirit, or John's revivalist role, Zechariah asks the practical question since, as he puts it, "My wife and I are very old" (1:18). The angel, huffily, replies, "I am Gabriel. I stand in God's presence" (1:19). Who are you, he asks, to doubt me?

In antiquity, the Gospel was not read by most people, in part because copying books was expensive, and in part because most people were illiterate. Instead, the Gospel was performed. We can

picture the speaker, demonstrating angelic exasperation, wondering how he will deal with this obtuse priest.

Gabriel explains: he is bringing "good news" (1:19). The Greek is from the term *euangelion*, with *eu* meaning "good," as in "euphemism" and "eulogy"; *angelion* is from the same root as *angel*, "messenger." This term, which underlies "evangelist" and "evangelical," comes into Middle English as "gospel," good news or good story. The term was a common one in antiquity; the *euangelion* of the empire could be a tax relief or a parade. From the city of Priene in Western Turkey we have from 9 BCE (I have to tell my students that the inscription does not actually read "9 BCE") an inscription that celebrates the birth of Augustus Caesar as "good news" (*euangelion*), calls Augustus a "savior both for us and for our descendants," and as if in anticipation of the Christmas story, speaks of how "the birthday of the god Augustus was the beginning of good news for the world."

Therefore, when we hear the "gospel" or meet an "evangelical," we need to ask: what is the good news that you bring? The good news here in Luke's first chapter is not just about the conception, birth, and public role of John, or even the birth of Jesus; the good news includes these stories and more, through to reports of Jesus' resurrection, in written form. It is the story Jesus' followers will remember and repeat.

The angel then explains that because the priest doubted this good news, "you will remain silent, unable to speak until the day when these things happen" (1:20). I imagine that at this point, words failed Zechariah. He was terrified and traumatized. Everything for which he had prayed will come to pass, but he is stuck between belief and doubt. What at this point can he say?

Often attributed to Saint Francis of Assisi is the advice, "Preach the gospel at all times. And if necessary, use words." How do we explain a revelation? How do we express the inexpressible? How does

the experience of the holy change our actions? our life? To proclaim the gospel requires words, but words without action are not signs of the Spirit; they are just wind. At the end of his story, Zechariah will find the words, but they will be, appropriately, prophetic poetry.

Meanwhile, the people are waiting; whenever clergy run late, people notice and, usually, complain. When Zechariah finally does appear, he cannot speak. The people "realized he had seen a vision in the temple" (1:22a). How they came to this realization Luke does not state, although the notice "he gestured to them" (1:22b) suggests that he used hand motions to describe this vision. What a strange game of charades, to express concepts such as "angel" and "pregnancy" and "turning." People in the late first century, watching the Gospel of Luke performed, would be laughing. Try explaining, through hand motions, the angelic vision yourselves, and then try not to smile.

Elizabeth's Pregnancy

Zechariah returns home. One could speculate, but I shall not, on how he explained his vision to Elizabeth. Thankfully, as we soon see, Elizabeth could read, so perhaps he wrote down the details.

Luke, again discreetly, mentions Elizabeth's pregnancy. For five months, that is, into her second trimester and showing, Elizabeth "kept to herself" (1:24). Luke gives no explanation for this behavior, but we can speculate: Was she afraid of miscarriage? Was she afraid that, before she had that baby bump, people would not believe she was pregnant?

That five-month marker also gives us alternative timing, and so we are back to the question of time and space. We have moved from "the days of King Herod" to "the time of the incense offering" to "five months" of pregnancy. From the political to the sacerdotal to the maternal: How do we mark time? Year of graduation? of marriage?

when children were born? before and after the death of a beloved? Do we keep looking at our watches? Is the time going too slowly or too quickly? Do we take the time to do what needs to be done?

Elizabeth recognizes that conception is a gift from God, who "has shown his favor to me by removing my disgrace among other people" (1:25). The people did not look at her as sinful, but they may have pitied her.

The reference to disgrace also connects Elizabeth to the matriarchs. Sarah exclaims, "Who could have told Abraham that Sarah would nurse sons? But now I've given birth to a son when he was old!" (Genesis 21:7). When Rachel, jealous of her fertile sister Leah, finally gives birth, she states, "God has taken away my shame" (Genesis 30:23). Before giving birth to Samuel, Hannah endured the taunts of her fertile co-wife, Peninnah (1 Samuel 1:6). When Elkanah asks his wife, "Hannah, why are you crying? . . . Why won't you eat? What are you so sad? Aren't I worth more to you than ten sons?" (1 Samuel 1:8), Hannah gives no reply.

For women and men struggling with infertility, who have experienced miscarriages, and who so very much want a child, Elizabeth's story acknowledges their pain.

When I was in graduate school, many of my friends were getting married and having children. I planned: I should finish the dissertation; I need financial security; I should have a house and daycare. And I worried about fertility; would I have the same problems that my mother had? Sarah Elizabeth arrived when I was twenty-nine (with Ph.D. and employed at Swarthmore College); Jay and I were among the older parents among her nursery school cohort. She was named after my father, Saul, and my teacher in graduate school, Elizabeth Clark. Yet she also carries the names of two very strong women, Sarah and Elizabeth, who did the impossible.

For women and men struggling
with infertility, who have
experienced miscarriages,
and who so very much want
a child, Elizabeth's story
acknowledges their pain.

John's Birth

John's birth is a time for great rejoicing, not only by his parents, but also by their neighbors and relatives (Luke 1:57-58). These family members and friends remained with the new parents until the eighth day after the child's birth, when their son is circumcised and named. We do not have clear testimony from Jewish sources, until the eighth century, that naming took place on the eighth day. It is possible that Luke preserves an earlier Jewish tradition. Remarkably, on occasion, the New Testament provides the background to Jewish history, rather than the other way around.

The plan was to name the child Zechariah after his father (1:59). King Herod had a number of children also named Herod, including some whom Luke mentions: Herod Antipas (who beheaded John), Herod Agrippa I (who killed James), and Herod Agrippa II (who heard Paul's defense but did not set him free).

A new time, a new practice, begins when Elizabeth insists, "No, his name will be John" (1:60). She speaks because the father, Zechariah, is still mute. The friends and relatives, not willing to accept Elizabeth's assertion since John is not a family name, motion to Zechariah; the motioning suggests that Zechariah is not only mute but also deaf. They doubt the woman. We find the same motif at the end of Luke's Gospel (24:10-11), when the women report seeing the empty tomb and the message from two "men" in dazzling clothes. The men do not believe them. They should have learned.

The tradition in Eastern European Judaism, Ashkenazic Judaism, is to name a child after a deceased relative to keep the memory alive. My name, Amy, is for my father's mother, Amelia. Jill is after my mother's father, Jacob. My parents always called me Amy-Jill to make sure that my father's mother and my mother's father would be remembered. Our son, Alexander David, is named for Jay's Aunt Elsie,

who had no children of her own, and for my maternal grandmother, Deborah known as Dora.

Luke prompts us: Do we know the meaning of our names? Were we named after a relative or family friend? after a politician or a movie star, a scientist or an author? Whose memory does our name keep alive, and whose memories do we cherish and honor? In whose memory do we act?

Zechariah confirms his wife's announcement. He asks for a writing tablet and writes, "His name is John" (1:63). Luke tells us that all were amazed. What I find amazing is the impression that everyone present was literate (sometimes being a historian can detract from the appreciation of the narrative). Luke does tend to give major figures an educational upgrade.

Zechariah's Song

Only now does Zechariah speak; he sings his praise of God (1:64). The song is traditionally called the "Benedictus," Latin for "blessed," the opening word (1:68 NRSV). This speaking confirms the miracle of John's birth. No longer silent, Zechariah had found the words to express his joy.

He is not alone in rejoicing. "Everyone throughout the Judean highlands" begins to ponder the child's fate (1:65). For some parents, giving birth means the establishment of a college fund or plans for athletic expertise or piano lessons. Perhaps, Luke suggests by the newness of John's name, that we have to let children be themselves, not clones of us, and not, heaven forbid, the object through which we fulfill our own longings.

When Sarah was in high school, she had little interest in studying. She asked, "Why study for the A if I can get B-plusses without the work?" Her father and I, both academics, were flummoxed. We could not fathom someone not wanting the A. But Sarah said, "I'm not an

academic." Jay and I looked at each other and suddenly, happily, realized that Sarah was her own person. Children should be what they want to be. We can guide, but we cannot control. Sarah has her own, very successful career, and we could not be happier. We encouraged her to be herself and to pursue dreams that she dreamed. That's what John's parents did, for John did not follow his father into Temple service. He found another way of serving the community.

The Spirit appears again, this time to inspire Zechariah to prophesy. After nine months of silence, what a celebration he offers. He's not the first to sing in Luke's Gospel; his words follow Mary's Magnificat, which she sings to Elizabeth (Zechariah, silent, may have been taking notes). He will not be the last, for his song anticipates the brief hymn of Simeon in the Temple. The Nativity accounts are not just prose; they are poetry and song.

Luke tells us that Zechariah, filled with the Spirit (of course), "prophesied" (1:67) and in doing so provides the assurance that, despite the newness of the Christmas story, a rock-solid base secures an anchor. God is invested in history, from the international level to the personal one. This investment does not mean micromanaging, and it does not mean eliminating either free will or the role of nature, of wind and seas, droughts and blight. It means both concern for the world and all its inhabitants and support that this investment, the tradition of Torah and Gospel, will guide us toward the good.

Zechariah's prayer, like Mary's Magnificat, is less a prediction than an assurance: God has acted in the past, and those actions have repercussions for the present and the future. The verbs of the prayer are in the past tense: "Bless the Lord God of Israel," the priest exhorts, "because he has come to help and has delivered his people" (1:68). *He has delivered.* Zechariah the priest acknowledges what Jews then, and now, already know: we are a people delivered from slavery and exile. Slaves, then and now, understand freedom in a way that people never oppressed cannot; people in exile understand home in a way

that those who have never been displaced cannot. At the same time, Zechariah, like the Exodus story, prompts us to remember those who remain yet enslaved and displaced. That remembering, that learning from our own history, is part of God's investment in us. It is also part of our responsibility to each other.

Zechariah continues by recalling God's promises regarding "David's house" (1:69). The concern is a political one, for David is not only the sweet singer of psalms but also King David, the founder of Israel's monarchy. To evoke David is necessarily to contrast him with Herod. Luke refers to David as God's "servant" (Greek: *pais*, an alternative translation would be "child"). Whether we translate the term as "servant" or "child," we learn that David's rule is not classified by might but by meekness. This is the type of leadership Jesus will promote.

Zechariah's assurance that God has "brought salvation from our enemies / and from the power of all those who hate us" (1:71) may be difficult to accept, given our present times, when every day brings news of a new atrocity. I am writing this paragraph in the wake of a shooting in Poway, near San Diego, where a young man, taught in his church that Christians had replaced Jews in the history of salvation, and convinced by the Bible that Jews are damned Christ-killers who deserve death themselves, entered a synagogue and began to carry out what he thought was his divinely ordained mission. He was not the first person both to claim Jesus as Lord and to kill Jews as the way he demonstrated his faith; he will not be the last to misinterpret his text and his God.

Luke reminds us of the connections of the church and Israel; Zechariah calls the church to remember its origins. When Zechariah speaks of God's "holy covenant" (1:72) and of the "solemn pledge he made to our ancestor Abraham" (1:73), he insists that the covenant with the people Israel continues.

The covenant with Abraham has a both/and rather than an either/or focus: it is both for Jews and for gentiles, for in Abraham, "all the families of the earth will be blessed" (Genesis 12:3). And since we are part of the same covenantal system, we should have a sense of mutual responsibility.

Yet for that investment to remain secure, the assurance that "we would be rescued from the power of our enemies" (Luke 1:74) requires Christians to help: by recognizing the common heritage of church and synagogue, by acknowledging the ongoing covenant with the Jewish people, by avoiding anti-Jewish teaching and preaching. Only then, will we be better able to "serve him without fear" (1:74).

After the promise and the wish for the nation, Zechariah finally turns to his son. He refers to John as "child" (Greek: *paidion*), a synonym for *pais*. King David and John, soon to be known as the Baptizer, are connected, each with his own role and both part of the larger whole of salvation history. The two anticipate the child, waiting in Mary's womb, who will be born in the next chapter of that history, and this Gospel.

John will, like his father, continue the role of prophet (1:76), the teller of truths. The comment that he will "go before the Lord to prepare his way" is replete with meaning. Zechariah here anticipates Luke 3:4, where the evangelist introduces the adult John, "as it was written in the scroll of the words of Isaiah the prophet, / *A voice crying out in the wilderness: / 'Prepare the way for the Lord; / make his paths straight.'*" Isaiah's prophecy, in its original context, was a message of consolation to the exiles in Babylon; Isaiah 40 begins, "Comfort, comfort my people! says your God" (40:1), and moves to the celebratory: "A voice is crying out: / 'Clear the LORD's way in the desert! / Make a level highway in the wilderness for our God! . . . / The LORD's glory will appear, / and all humanity will see it together; / the LORD's mouth has commanded it" (40:3, 5). Build a highway in

the desert, Isaiah says, for your exile is coming to an end and you are about to return home.

By evoking Isaiah's prophecy, Luke is telling readers: I've given you the first verse of Isaiah 40, now fill in the rest of the Song. The Gospel writers consistently allude to Israel's Scriptures, and our reading is inevitably enriched if we recognize the allusions and then put the context of the original quote into conversation with its Gospel use. Zechariah, by alluding to Isaiah, reminds us of exile and return, of promise and fulfillment, of ancient Israel and the new movement to come.

And he does more. Luke's attentive readers would have noticed the "voice" that "is crying out" and the "LORD's mouth" and then recalled that Zechariah had been unable to speak. What are words worth? What are voices for? What will our mouths open to say?

For Luke, Isaiah's proclamation has new meaning: The "Lord" for Luke is Jesus of Nazareth, and the "way" to be prepared is not a literal highway in the desert, but the new movement that called itself not "Christian" but followers of "the Way" (see Acts 9:2). The sense of movement, of action, remains in the name. The people who will follow John, and from him to Jesus, will be known by walking the walk or, as John will express the point, "produce fruit that shows you have changed your hearts and lives" (Luke 3:8).

Zechariah's hymn highlights two more themes, along with the role of the Spirit, the attention to women's roles, and the connections to ancient Israel and the biblical tradition. First, Zechariah connects the work of John to the "forgiveness of their sins" (1:77). His attention is not on the cross, but on human interaction. Jews knew that God was always ready, and eager, to forgive anyone who repents. They also knew that repentance required correction: turning, as we have seen, means walking the right path. And John draws the map.

John tells those who come to him for immersion that the fruits they must bear consist in ethical action: "Whoever has two shirts

must share with the one who has none, and whoever has food must do the same" (3:11). So simple and so difficult.

Finally, Zechariah speaks of light to those who sit in darkness (1:79). His point is not a matter of theological proclamation; his point is that people really were in his time—and really are, in our time—sitting in darkness, "in the shadow of death." We have heard the words before, in the famous Psalm 23:4, "Yea, though I walk through the valley of the shadow of death, I will fear no evil: for thou art with me" (KJV). The image of darkness also appears in Isaiah 42:7, where Israel's role is "to open blind eyes, to lead the prisoners from prison, and those who sit in darkness from the dungeon." Rather than immediately spiritualize the language of light and darkness, Luke, echoing Isaiah, insists on attending to those who are in prison, behind bars, without daylight.

The sense of God's "deep compassion" (Luke 1:78) makes bearable that shadow and can allow us to find that "path of peace" (1:79). That insistence is how many behind bars continue to live.

We will not meet Zechariah and Elizabeth again in Luke's Gospel. But we know that they raised a child in the Jewish tradition. Perhaps he learned from this mother's example to insist on what he knew to be right, despite community pressure to the contrary. Perhaps he learned from his father the importance of asking the right questions and using the right words, of speaking up when cries of justice were needed to break the silence of complicity.

Chapter 1 of Luke's Gospel ends with the notice concerning John: "The child grew up, becoming strong in character. He was in the wilderness until he began his public ministry to Israel" (1:80). John will sit in the shadow of darkness. The psalmist sang, "You bathe my head in oil" (Psalm 23:5) while Herod Antipas will murder the Baptizer. Yet Zechariah's song suggests that John knew he had done what he was called to do. The cup did not pass for him, as it will not pass for Jesus. John lost his life, but his message will be remembered.

Chapter 2

THE PROMISE OF POTENTIAL

When Elizabeth was six months pregnant, God sent the angel Gabriel to Nazareth, a city in Galilee, to a virgin who was engaged to a man named Joseph, a descendant of David's house. The virgin's name was Mary. When the angel came to her, he said, "Rejoice, favored one! The Lord is with you!" She was confused by these words and wondered what kind of greeting this might be. The angel said, "Don't be afraid, Mary. God is honoring you. Look! You will conceive and give birth to a son, and you will name him Jesus. He will be great and he will be called the Son of the Most High. The Lord God will give him the throne of David his father. He will rule over Jacob's house forever, and there will be no end to his kingdom."

Then Mary said to the angel, "How will this happen since I haven't had sexual relations with a man?"

The angel replied, "The Holy Spirit will come over you and the power of the Most High will overshadow you. Therefore, the one who is to be born will be holy. He will be called God's Son. Look, even in her old age, your relative Elizabeth

*has conceived a son. This woman who was labeled 'unable to
conceive' is now six months pregnant. Nothing is impossible
for God."*

*Then Mary said, "I am the Lord's servant. Let it be with me
just as you have said." Then the angel left her.*

*Mary got up and hurried to a city in the Judean highlands.
She entered Zechariah's home and greeted Elizabeth. When
Elizabeth heard Mary's greeting, the child leaped in her
womb, and Elizabeth was filled with the Holy Spirit. With
a loud voice she blurted out, "God has blessed you above all
women, and he has blessed the child you carry. Why do I
have this honor, that the mother of my Lord should come to
me? As soon as I heard your greeting, the baby in my womb
jumped for joy. Happy is she who believed that the Lord
would fulfill the promises he made to her."*

Mary said,

> *"With all my heart I glorify the Lord!*
> > *In the depths of who I am I rejoice in God my savior.*
> *He has looked with favor on the low status of his servant.*
> > *Look! From now on, everyone will consider me
> > highly favored*
> > > *because the mighty one has done great things
> > > for me.*
> *Holy is his name.*
> > *He shows mercy to everyone,*
> > > *from one generation to the next,*
> > > *who honors him as God.*
> *He has shown strength with his arm.*
> > *He has scattered those with arrogant thoughts and
> > proud inclinations.*
> > *He has pulled the powerful down from their thrones
> > and lifted up the lowly.*

He has filled the hungry with good things
and sent the rich away empty-handed.
He has come to the aid of his servant Israel,
remembering his mercy,
just as he promised to our ancestors,
to Abraham and to Abraham's descendants
forever."

Mary stayed with Elizabeth about three months, and then
returned to her home.

Luke 1:26-56

Why Mary Matters

I've always been attracted to Mary. I have a particular attachment
to Our Lady of Fatima because I grew up in a Portuguese neighbor-
hood where the story of her appearance to three children in 1917
was celebrated. One of my favorite movies is the 1952 *Miracle of Our
Lady of Fatima.* When I was younger, I was torn between wanting
to have a vision of the Blessed Virgin and become a nun like Sister
Lucia, or wanting to elope with Gilbert Roland, the male lead.

Mary's mother, St. Anne, also impressed me. When I was a child
my parents took me to Quebec, where we visited the Basilica of
Sainte-Anne-de-Beaupré. I can still picture the crutches and wheel-
chairs and canes left by pilgrims who found healing. My mother's
name was Anne, and for a while I connected St. Anne and my mother
because, like St. Anne, my mother had fertility problems and then
finally, when no one expected it, she gave birth to a daughter.

From those childhood memories, my appreciation of Mary has
grown. Each of the four Gospel portraits of her opens to multiple
insights, from the concerned mother in Mark, who fears that her son,
performing exorcisms and associating with tax collectors, is getting a
bad reputation; to the young woman in Matthew, whose betrothed,

Joseph, decides to divorce her upon discovering that she is pregnant; to the courageous woman in Luke, who receives an annunciation that she will become pregnant with David's heir, who visits her cousin Elizabeth, and who exults in the Magnificat, a hymn of praise and revolution; to John's unnamed "mother of Jesus," who intercedes with him for wine at the wedding in Cana, and who stands at the cross where she witnesses his death. Mary appears in Acts as well, where she is counted among the faithful in Jerusalem. Stories about her continued to develop in antiquity, including the second-century *Protevangelium of James*, where we first meet her parents, Anna and Joachim, and read of her childhood in the Temple, her chaste marriage to the elderly Joseph, and the birth of Jesus so miraculous that Mary remained a virgin post-partum.

In this chapter, we look at Mary's encounter with the angel Gabriel, her visit to her cousin Elizabeth, and her magnificent Magnificat, all in the Gospel of Luke. We also see how understanding both historical context and literary connections—the connotations of her name, her place in the annunciation scenes in the Scriptures of Israel, and the meaning of the Magnificat in light of Roman domination—adds profound implications to the narratives.

The Name *Mary*

In chapter 1, we saw how Zechariah's name, based in the Hebrew word for "remember," helps us draw the connections between Israel's story and the new story about to unfold. We saw how Elizabeth's name, referring to God's fidelity to promises made, portends fulfillment of the ancient covenants. And we saw how John's name, the Hebrew *Yochanan*, meaning "God is gracious," fits with the one who will come in the power of the Spirit and in the role of Elijah, to reconcile families and proclaim the messianic age.

Mary's name also has symbolic value. First, she reminds us of

Miriam, the clever and courageous sister of Moses. The Egyptian ruler, Pharaoh, had become concerned that the Israelites, an immigrant people, had become too numerous. First, he enslaved them, and then he ordered that the midwives kill all the boys at birth. When the midwives refused, with the ruse that the Israelite women were so strong that they gave birth without their aid, Pharaoh "gave an order to all his people: 'Throw every baby boy born to the Hebrews into the Nile River, but you can let all the girls live'" (Exodus 1:22).

Knowing that she could not keep her son hidden, Moses's mother places him in an ark (yes, "ark," the same Hebrew word used for Noah's boat) and floats him down the Nile, in the hopes that an Egyptian will find him and protect him. Pharaoh's daughter, coming to the river to bathe, spots the baby, takes pity on him, and rescues him. It was Miriam, identified in Exodus 1 only as "his sister," who suggests, "Would you like me to go and find one of the Hebrew women to nurse the child for you?" (2:7). The princess agrees, and so Moses was nursed at his own mother's breast. Mary's parents, knowing this story, might have named their daughter after Miriam, who cared for her family, and who knew how both to protect and to negotiate.

Miriam's guidance continues at the Exodus: "Then the prophet Miriam, Aaron's sister, took a tambourine in her hand. All the women followed her playing tambourines and dancing" (15:20). Miriam is the first woman in the Bible called a "prophet"; up to this point in the biblical story, only Abraham and Aaron are accorded this title. Her prophecy is one of proclamation rather than prediction: "Sing to the LORD, for an overflowing victory! / Horse and rider he threw into the sea!" (15:21). Although Exodus 15:1 ascribes this same line to Moses and although today we speak of the "Song of Moses," I suspect Miriam sang it first, for women in Israel's Scriptures, women such as Deborah and Hannah, are the keepers of songs. (This would not be the first time that a man got the credit for a woman's work. I suspect

my feminist credentials are showing.)

Miriam is remembered primarily as poet and prophet and protector, and not as wife and mother. Mary, the mother of Jesus, is remembered primarily because of her son, but her motherhood is not her only characteristic. She, too, is poet and prophet and protector. When the "woman in the crowd spoke up [to Jesus]: 'Happy is the mother who gave birth to you and who nursed you,'" he responded, "Happy rather are those who hear God's word and put it into practice" (Luke 11:27-28). His response is both general and particular, for Mary his mother epitomizes those who hear and obey.

By the first century, Mary is the most common name among Jewish women in Judea and Galilee. The New Testament mentions numerous Marys: Mary the mother of Jesus, Mary Magdalene, Mary the sister of Martha, Mary the mother of John Mark, and Mary mentioned as one of Paul's friends in Romans 16.

It is possible they were named not only after Miriam the sister of Moses but also after Mariamne, the Hasmonean wife of Herod the Great. In the first centuries BCE and CE, some Jews still sought the return of the Hasmonean kingship, the indigenous Jewish kingship, rather than a Roman appointee. Marrying a woman from the Hasmonean lineage helped Herod secure his throne; plus, Josephus reports that Herod loved her.

Miriam and Mariamne both stand behind Mary the mother of Jesus. I can imagine Mary telling her son stories of Moses and the Maccabees, of freedom from Egyptian slavery and the rededication of the Temple at Hanukkah. She would have told him about advocating for others and about leading by song rather than by sword.

We might finally pay attention to how names change. In Luke 1:27, Gabriel speaks to "Miriam," which is how Mary appears in Greek, and the mother of Jesus remains "Miriam" throughout Luke's infancy materials. But Luke speaks of "Maria," not "Miriam," when

he talks about Mary Magdalene. Mary the sister of Martha is in the Greek "Miriam." The Aramaic beneath all these names would have been Maryam. What is lost, and gained, when names change to fit new cultures?

Mary's Background

Although we have two genealogies for Joseph, the Gospels do not identify Mary's parents or name any siblings. But for Mary's actual background, we simply don't know. I appreciate the textual silence. While genealogies tell us something of who we are (and now, DNA testing can tell us more), we are finally responsible for our own stories.

Later writers filled in the background. The *Protevangelium* (literally, "pre-gospel") *of James*, recalls Abraham and Sarah, and Elizabeth and Zechariah, in describing Anna and Joachim, a righteous, elderly, and infertile couple. Their prayer is heard; they have a child, but in this case, the child is a daughter. Now following the story of Hannah in 1 Samuel, Anna (the connection between the names is not accidental) vows to dedicate her daughter to God. When Mary turns three, her parents bring her to live in the Jerusalem Temple. The Temple was many things, but it was not a daycare; such details should not, however, get in the way of a good story.

When Mary turns twelve (and so old enough to menstruate), the priests determine to find a man to protect her and to bring her to his home. They call righteous widowers, among them Joseph, here seen as elderly and with grown children. The "James" in the title is James the brother of Jesus, here imagined to be a child of Joseph by a previous marriage. When Joseph's walking stick begins to flower, the priests realize he is divinely chosen to care for Mary.

The story continues with numerous details. It recounts how Mary and her virgin companions spin the thread for the Temple veil,

When we do not have details and want to know more, we tell stories. Such stories and others about Mary resemble Midrash, Jewish storytelling that fills in gaps.... Good stories always give rise to more stories.

and it was while spinning that she encounters the angel Gabriel. Following the stories of Joseph's concern that Mary had been unfaithful (Matthew 1) and of the census (Luke 2), it depicts the birth of Jesus not in a house (Matthew) or a stable (Luke), but in a cave. This is the legend that lies behind the grotto in the Church of the Nativity in Bethlehem. There, a midwife proclaims that following the birth, Mary has remained a virgin. Turning to the story of the Slaughter of the Innocents (Matthew 2), the *Protevangelium* reports that Elizabeth and baby John escape the Roman soldiers when a mountain miraculously hides them, but the soldiers kill Zechariah.

When we do not have details and want to know more, we tell stories. Such stories and others about Mary resemble Midrash, Jewish storytelling that fills in gaps: What was Moses's childhood in Pharaoh's house like? What did Zipporah tell Miriam? And so on. Good stories always give rise to more stories.

The Annunciation

In Matthew's Gospel, as we see in the next chapter, Joseph dreams dreams that inform him about Mary's pregnancy. Luke keeps the spotlight on Mary herself. The Gospels thus provide two different perspectives. As we've seen, theologically profound stories require more than one iteration and more than one perspective.

We've already heard one annunciation in Luke's Gospel: the angel's promise to Zechariah that he and Elizabeth would have a child in their old age. The story repeats a motif we see over and over again in Israel's Scriptures. Like variations on a theme, it resounds.

The annunciation is a literary convention, and readers are to delight in the variations: Who makes the annunciation? Is the woman pregnant or not? Is the focus on the father, the mother, or the child? How does the woman learn about her pregnancy? When I was a child the convention on television was the Western: *High Chaparral*,

Bonanza, *Big Valley*, *The Virginian*, and movies with John Wayne. Now we have shows with letters, such as *NCIS*, *CSI*, along with variations of *Law and Order*. These conventions tap into the human imagination and speak to human longings. The television shows do that for entertainment; the Bible, by repeating stories, does more. It not only entertains but also instructs, inspires, and even more, astounds.

First is an angel's appearance to Hagar, the Egyptian slave, already pregnant with Ishmael, informing her that God has recognized her affliction and that God will protect and bless her son (Genesis 16). In Israel's Scriptures, God's concern is not restricted to insiders: it extends to strangers, to slaves, to women, and to any who are oppressed, for we are all children of God. The angel's next appearance is to Abraham, with Sarah overhearing the news and laughing at the thought that she would have a child given her age and Abraham's age (Genesis 18). Rebecca, who had already suffered from infertility, finally conceives, but as the pregnancy becomes increasingly difficult, she cries out to God. The announcement she receives is that two nations in her womb are at war and that the older (Esau) will serve the younger (Jacob) (Genesis 25).

In Judges 13, the wife of Manoah, also infertile, encounters an angel in the field, who announces that she will conceive and who then gives her some good prenatal advice about avoiding alcohol. When Mrs. Manoah reports the encounter to her husband, he asks that she get him the next time the angel appears. He may well have been thinking: *Handsome man in the field, out of sight, and now she's pregnant?* The child turns out to be the judge Samson. Then Hannah, taunted by her husband's fertile co-wife, prays for a child in the temple at Shiloh. Here the priest Eli tells her that she will conceive; it is Hannah's story that underlies the *Protevangelium*. By the time we get to the Great Woman (yes, that's what's she's called) of Shunem,

who is without a child and with an older husband, we know what is going to happen without any angelic or prophetic word (2 Kings 4). Luke continues the tradition with the annunciation to Zechariah. But now we come to the most miraculous annunciation of them all.

The story begins with the notice that "when Elizabeth was six months pregnant, God sent the angel Gabriel to Nazareth, a city in Galilee" (Luke 1:26). The single verse overflows with meaning. First is, again, the matter of time. The "sixth" month does not mean June; it refers to the sixth month of Elizabeth's pregnancy. We saw in the last chapter how Elizabeth had hidden herself for five months (1:24); she's now proudly showing. The notice also anticipates the end of Mary's meeting with the angel, for Gabriel states that the proof of his annunciation is Elizabeth's pregnancy. Thus, the *sixth month* in 1:26 and his assurance that "even in her old age, your relative Elizabeth has conceived a son. [and] is now six months pregnant" in 1:36 frame the story.

We have already met Gabriel before, as he announced the conception and birth of John. Luke, the excellent storyteller, has primed us to expect the angel to be impatient and not one to appreciate questions. We shall be pleasantly surprised, and relieved. The angel's biblical role to this point has been to explain to Daniel his visions (Daniel 8:16; 9:21). The trumpet, which appears so often in the Book of Revelation that one can hear an orchestra, announces the end of the world: "The trumpet will blast, and the dead will be raised with bodies that won't decay" (1 Corinthians 15:52). Yet we can certainly hear, if we listen closely, trumpets sounding when the angel appears to Mary.

Gabriel is sent by God, who remains active in history, in time and space. He is sent to Nazareth in Galilee, which is Luke's way of helping readers, who may have no sense where Nazareth is, to locate it geographically. We are no longer in Judea or in the environs

of Jerusalem, and we are no longer under direct Roman occupation. We are in Nazareth, a place so small that the Gospels are the first sources to mention it. Nazareth is a small village of maybe a few hundred people.

What an amazing verse: in just a few words, Luke 1:26 sets the time and place, offers a heavenly messenger and a divine intervention into history, connects the celestial and the terrestrial, and anticipates a good story to come. We are not disappointed. Indeed, every verse in this chapter is replete with meaning, if only we had the time to do more in-depth study.

God sends the angel to "a virgin who was engaged to a man named Joseph, a descendant of David's house. The virgin's name was Mary" (Luke 1:27). That is the word order of the Greek. I'd like to think that Luke was using the literary technique known as "end-stress," where the most important part of the story comes at the end. We can watch the build-up in terms of importance. First is the virgin. We remember Gabriel's words to Zechariah, so we know that conception is in the air. Thus, we wonder: how is this virgin to be a mother? Second is the notice of her engagement; she is in a legal relationship. Will the man be the father?

Third, the name *Joseph*. Luke has told us in the opening verses that others had already told the story of Jesus, and so Luke may be assuming that readers of this Gospel have already read Matthew's story. Matthew's first and second chapters focus on Joseph's story; Luke tells what will be Mary's story. Assuring us that Joseph is from the Davidic line, Luke reminds us of God's promises to David, "When the time comes for you to die and you lie down with your ancestors, I will raise up your descendant—one of your very own children—to succeed you, and I will establish his kingdom. He will build a temple for my name, and I will establish his royal throne forever" (2 Samuel 7:12-13). As Elizabeth's name indicates, God is faithful to promises

made. Finally, at the culmination of the verse, comes Mary's name. Our attention is not only to her virginal status, her marriage to Joseph, and the Davidic lineage; our attention is also on the woman, Mary, and the choices she will have to make.

Historically, Mary would be in her late teens because that is when, as best as we can determine, Jewish women in Judea and Galilee married in the late Second Temple period. Joseph, unless we read with the *Protevangelium*, would be about ten years older.

To this young woman Gabriel announces, "Greetings, favored one! The Lord is with you" (Luke 1:28 NRSV). The Greek for "Greetings" is *chaire*, which was the standard greeting at the time and connotes rejoicing, as in the English, "Glad to meet you." In various grammatical forms, the Greek word shows up almost seventy times in the New Testament; its first appearance coincides with the star of Bethlehem, for the Magi: "When they saw the star, they rejoiced [*echaresan*] with exceeding great joy [*charan*]" (Matthew 2:10 KJV). The term also echoes Luke 1:14, where the angel told Zechariah, "He will be a joy and delight to you, and many people will rejoice [*charesontai*] at his birth." The story is one where gladness abounds. In Latin, the term is *Ave*, literally, "be well" or "hail," and from the Latin *Ave Maria* we eventually get to the English "Hail Mary."

Gabriel's next comment, "The Lord is with you," is both comforting and ominous. When an angel comes to an individual to make an announcement, there's both the assurance of divine protection and, usually, a catch. An angelic visit—whether to announce a baby or a commission or to interpret a vision—typically requires a response. God told Abraham to leave his home and family to go to Canaan; God told Moses to demand that Pharaoh set the Israelite slaves free; and God told Jonah to prophesy, and he attempted to run away. God asks a lot. God also gives us the strength to respond.

My divinity students will sometimes invite me to their ordina-

When an angel comes to
an individual to make an
announcement, there's both the
assurance of divine protection
and, usually, a catch. An angelic
visit—whether to announce
a baby or a commission or to
interpret a vision—typically
requires a response.

tions. The occasion is joyful, and at the same time I think: this is a really hard road, or a narrow path, that they have chosen. That's why we speak of vocations, of being "called" by the divine to a life of service. The congregation sings Dan Schutte's hymn—"Here I am, Lord. Is it I, Lord?"[1]—and I think of all those called, including Abraham and Moses, Deborah and Miriam, and now Mary. It will not be an easy life. Not all who are called respond.

Luke tells us that Mary was "much perplexed by his words and pondered what sort of greeting this might be" (Luke 1:29 NRSV). The Greek for "perplexed" is *diatarasso*, which connotes not just confusion, but terror. As we've seen, this is the same root that describes Herod's fear upon hearing of a rival king (Matthew 2:3) and Zechariah's fear upon seeing the angel in the Temple (Luke 1:12). Something momentous and life-changing is about to occur to a Jewish woman on the outskirts of the empire.

Assuring her not to fear, the angel tells Mary, "God is honoring you" (1:30). Brilliantly, Luke does not record what prompts this favor. There is no indication that Mary got divine notice because she helped her mother with the laundry, did well in school, had a beautiful singing voice, was pretty, prayed a lot, or was a virgin. We can fill in reasons if we want, but I prefer the readings that just let God be free to choose whomever: a fisherman, a cloth dyer, a tent maker, anyone.

Now comes the catch. The angel tells her that she will conceive and bear a son, to be named Jesus. He will be the "Son of the Most High"; not only will he inherit David's throne, but also he will reign over an eternal kingdom (Luke 1:31-33). That's a lot to take in.

We've already noted the political implications of Mary's name: Miriam the prophet who demanded equal access to God; Mariamne the princess who represented independence from Rome. Now she hears of the restoration of David's kingdom. The Gospels continually ask: Which king do you follow? Where is your worship directed?

What do you proclaim?

Were I Mary, I might have asked: What do you intend to do with the Romans? Or how is my son to accomplish these goals? Mary starts with the practical, not the political: "How will this happen since I haven't had sexual relations with a man?" (1:34). The Greek is *parthenos*, "virgin."

On the CEB translation, a story: a good friend mentioned to me that her sister and her niece had heard me speak on a television show about Mary's virginity. The niece, eight years old or so, asked her mother, "What's a virgin?" My first thought was, "Did she never sing 'Silent Night'?" Or did she think that the song was about a pudgy fellow named "Round John Virgin"? Perhaps the bluntness of the CEB translation is what we need.

Given the angel's somewhat huffy response to Zechariah, and his striking the priest mute for asking a question, I might have expected something similar here. But no, the angel responds with a theologically profound proclamation: "The Holy Spirit will come over you and the power of the Most High will overshadow you. Therefore, the one who is to be born will be holy. He will be called God's Son" (1:35). Luke is not interested in the how, the mechanism; Luke is interested in the what, the action of the Spirit, whose presence flows throughout the Gospel and Acts. And, as we'll see, rather than being struck mute, Mary in Zechariah's house will burst forth in song.

Luke may be hinting at something more. Luke's version of Jesus' genealogy starts with Jesus and backtracks to "son of Enos son of Seth son of Adam son of God" (3:38). One way of reading this genealogy is to see that we are all, as children of Adam, also children of God. We are therefore all animated by the Spirit of God. The angel's words to Mary both differentiate Jesus by predicting his everlasting kingdom and connect him to humanity, surprisingly but beautifully, with the title "God's Son."

Continuing the remarkable nature of this prophecy is its cultural resonances. Jews knew that we are all children of God. Deuteronomy 14:1 proclaims to the Israelites, "You are the Lord's children" (Hebrew: *b'nai atem l'YHWH elohechem*). In 1 Kings 8:25, Solomon, as if anticipating Luke's Gospel, prays, "So now, Lord, Israel's God, keep what you promised my father David, your servant, when you said to him, 'You will never fail to have a successor sitting on Israel's throne as long as your descendants carefully walk before me just as you walked before me.'" Wisdom 5:5, from the Old Testament Apocrypha/Deuterocanonical Texts, speaks of the repentant who are "God's children" and are "considered one of the saints." Perhaps best known, Jesus tells his disciples, "Happy are people who make peace, because they will be called God's children" (Matthew 5:9). For Jews, God is the heavenly father, and we are his children. That is why Jews, like Jesus, and why Jesus' followers address God as "father."

Not so much in the pagan world. There, along with heroes such as Hercules, Perseus, and Theseus, and brilliant men such as Pythagoras, divine sons tended to be emperors: Julius Caesar, his heir Augustus, Tiberias, Nero, Domitian, and so on. For example, Virgil, whom people would know from the *Aeneid*, described Augustus Caesar as the "son of a God who shall set up the golden age."

In Luke's view, coming from the Jewish rather than the pagan sensibilities, we are all children of God. Therefore, those who say that the Nativity stories are mythological claptrap have missed the main point. The main point in this Gospel is not the technicality of Jesus' conception, and belief in the virginal conception (we only get a virgin "birth" in the *Protevangelium*) should not be a litmus test to determine who is a "Christian." Luke has a much more important story to tell: about divine care and human potential, about how we are all children of God and can therefore do God's will, about the difficult choices we must make, about our memories and our goals.

Before Mary has a chance to question further, Gabriel announces the proof of his prediction. Mary does not ask for a sign, but she receives one: "your relative Elizabeth has conceived a son. This woman who was labeled 'unable to conceive' is now six months pregnant" (Luke 1:36). The sign could have been anything: a shooting star or rainbow, a plant that blooms out of season, or a tree that gives fruit in abundance; anything can be a sign, if we are open to interpretation. This sign is the good news of Elizabeth's pregnancy.

The angel's final comment is, "Nothing is impossible for God" (1:37). In the biological scheme of things, conception to a virgin is seen as more miraculous than conception to a woman presumed to have gone through menopause. But I prefer to take the entire story as more than a gynecological report. What is not impossible? It is not impossible that God could call us, indeed has called us, no matter our place or family of birth, economic status, or gender. It is not impossible that we can imagine a heavenly kingdom on earth, ruled by justice and compassion rather than by sword. It is not impossible that we can not only remember but also be inspired by our past stories and tell them, even live them, anew.

The claim that nothing is impossible for God gives rise to annoying philosophical questions, such as, "Can God make a rock so heavy that God can't lift it?" On a more serious note, the idea that nothing is impossible with God can be a very difficult statement because it can give the impression that God *could have* acted when we needed healing or rescue. The biblical story is less a matter of miraculous rescue than it is of human response to situations for which rescue is needed: the response to slavery, to exile, to genocide. It was the faith of ancient Israel, and of the early followers of Jesus, that allowed them to survive the passing of time and the dispersal throughout the world.

And it is not impossible that we can respond, as Mary did, "Here am I" (1:38 NRSV; the Greek is *idou*, usually translated "behold").

"Look at me," Mary says. "See me, pay attention to me." But look at me not because I am a queen on a throne. No, "I am the Lord's servant." The Greek for "servant" is *doule*, literally, "slave." Claiming the identity of a slave can be difficult, even traumatic, for people who have a history of being enslaved, whether Israelites in Egypt, Africans who were brought in chains through the Middle Passage, or people who are trafficked even today. For some readers, the idea of being a "slave of the Lord" is liberating because it proclaims that one is free from any human master. Her self-description also anticipates Jesus' own form of leadership: not to lord it over, but to serve. As he tells his disciples, "whoever wants to be first among you will be your slave" (Matthew 20:27).

The title "slave"—usually translated "servant" when predicated of Moses, Paul, and others—would not have sounded so genteel in a first-century context, when actual slaves were hearing this story. For them to find a connection to Mary may have given them hope.

Mary and Elizabeth

Already pregnant—Luke does not bother with the details, and neither should we—Mary hastens to visit Elizabeth (Luke 1:39). The haste is not because she is pregnant out of wedlock and fears being stoned. Such readings of Luke and Matthew come from historical ignorance. Even the story of the woman caught in adultery in John 8, where Jesus advises, "Whoever hasn't sinned should throw the first stone" (8:7), does not presume that anyone present is actually carrying a stone. The question about how to address the adultery is an honor challenge: were Jesus to say, "Stone her," his opponents would accuse him of barbarism. Were he to say, "Don't stone her," they'd ask him by what authority he could make such a pronouncement. Mary is not in danger of capital punishment.

She goes with haste to Elizabeth, since it is already Elizabeth's sixth month of pregnancy. I also think she goes because she needs Elizabeth. As we've seen, the Gospels tell us nothing of Mary's parents. Perhaps Mary, newly pregnant, needs an older woman, a trusted relative, with whom she can share her feelings, both physical and spiritual.

The house to which Mary travels belongs to Zechariah, but Mary greets not him, but Elizabeth (Luke 1:40). We can sense the excitement in that meeting: the two women with unexpected but wanted pregnancies anticipating a new future. I imagine Mary later greeted Zechariah, but Luke lingers on the meeting of the two women. They remind me of Ruth and Naomi, cleaving together, celebrating family.

The excitement grows. We do not hear Mary's words; these are reserved for Elizabeth. But we do hear of the reaction to them. Not only did Elizabeth hear Mary's greeting, but also Elizabeth's child heard. At the sound of the younger woman's voice, Elizabeth, in her sixth month, felt the baby move (1:41).

The notice of the baby's movement will become the frame for Elizabeth's praise of Mary. To this feeling in her womb, Elizabeth is, like many in Luke's Gospel, "filled with the Holy Spirit" (1:41), and it is her sense of divine presence, of something moving in the air that inspires her, that prompts her to exclaim, "God has blessed you above all women, and he has blessed the child you carry" (1:42). Words of blessing appear over five hundred times in the Bible. The first time *blessed* appears in the New Testament is in the Sermon on the Mount ("Blessed are the poor in spirit, for theirs is the kingdom of heaven" [Matthew 5:3 NRSV]), but Elizabeth's exultation is its first appearance in Luke's Gospel. From here it will be repeated again by Elizabeth, by Mary herself, by Simeon upon seeing the baby Jesus, and then by Jesus, often. The text now becomes filled not only with joy but also with blessing.

Words of blessing appear over five hundred times in the Bible. The first time *blessed* appears in the New Testament is in the Sermon on the Mount, but Elizabeth's exultation is its first appearance in Luke's Gospel.

Elizabeth not only feels the blessing in her body but also sees it in Mary, whom she calls "the mother of my Lord" (Luke 1:43). Unless Mary's greeting contained the information that she was pregnant also, then Elizabeth is offering a prophetic word on multiple levels. First, she is the first to announce her cousin's pregnancy, before Mary was likely showing. There is no five months of hiding here. Perhaps Elizabeth was the one to confirm Mary's own pregnancy. Just as Elizabeth's child is a sign to Mary of the truth of the angel's words, so Elizabeth confirms the angel's words by noting Mary's pregnancy. This would not be the first time a wise, older woman mentioned to a young friend or relative, "I think you're pregnant."

Second, Elizabeth knows that Mary carries not just a beloved child but the heir of David. I doubt most mothers would say to another: "Your child is more important than mine": clearly, the Spirit is at work here.

Elizabeth confirms her prophecy by telling Mary what we readers already know: that Mary's voice, her greeting, caused the child to jump for joy (1:44). Elizabeth's last words in the Gospel are to bestow a blessing on Mary: "Blessed is she who believed that there would be a fulfillment of what was spoken to her by the Lord" (1:45 NRSV). Again, we did not hear Mary's greeting, which could have been as simple as the angel's greeting to her, *chaire*. Luke suggests that Elizabeth, through prophetic insight, discerned the message and celebrated the hope.

The visit is in part a story about hearing. The greeting that both mother and baby hear prompts action and joy. Words matter, and the sound of words matters. In ancient Israel, the ear rather than the eye was the locus of revelation. God creates by speaking, "Let there be light" (Genesis 1:3). The watchword is "Israel, listen! Our God is the Lord!" (Deuteronomy 6:4), and the Gospel of John, repeating the

sounds of Genesis, begins, "In the beginning was the Word" (John 1:1). In an age in which literacy was low and books expensive, one listened to stories. Words have meaning and power. That's why Jesus keeps saying, "Let the person who has ears, listen."

The Magnificat

Elizabeth had blessed Mary for believing the angel's words. Mary extends that blessing from Elizabeth's lips to the voice of the world: "Everyone will consider me highly favored" (Luke 1:48 CEB), or, closer to the Greek: "All generations shall call me blessed" (KJV). The CEB translation would be more congenial to a number of my Protestant students, who find Mary to be a stumbling block. They do not want to think of her as an intercessor or as the Queen of Heaven.

Mary's Magnificat, together with her words to Gabriel and Elizabeth's words to her, explains why she should be blessed, even by Protestants. She was able to receive the angel's words and to accept them with both humility and grace. We see through her prayer, the Magnificat, that her focus is not on herself; it is on the mighty acts of God.

Mary begins, "With all my heart, I glorify the Lord!" (1:46 CEB), although the Greek is "with all my soul [*psyche*]." She praises with her being. Every single part of her blesses. The CEB reads, "In the depths of who I am I rejoice in God my savior," although the Greek in verse 47 for "in the depths of who I am" is "my spirit [*pneuma*]." It's the same Greek word used for the Holy Spirit, so the Holy Spirit and the human spirit unite.

The union is rejoicing for "God my savior." *Savior* is the right word; the Greek term here is *soter*, as in "soteriology," the technical term for discussions of salvation. For the Jewish Scriptures and for Jews in antiquity, salvation is less an eschatological matter of getting

into heaven or having eternal life; nor is it a matter of forgiveness of sin, since they knew that God always forgave the repentant sinner. Salvation means freedom or release from current circumstances: slavery, poverty, ill health, hunger, and thirst. In her song, Mary is talking about salvation in the past and the present, not about the far future. She can feel that salvation, in her body, in her soul, in her spirit, and in her womb. She can feel it because she knows that God has "looked with favor on the low status of his servant" (1:48), and it is for that reason—because God noticed her in her humility—that she will be considered "blessed."

Mary then proclaims God's name to be holy (1:49). As her slave-status anticipates Jesus' form of leadership through serving, her proclamation here anticipates Jesus' prayer, "Holy is his name." As with father-language, we again find traditional Jewish piety. The divine name, so holy that YHWH cannot be pronounced and so that the name should not be taken frivolously, shows again the importance of how we are identified. This "hallowing of the divine name" is not taken with the seriousness it deserves. In first grade, in the local public elementary school, we recited this prayer (I've now given you a sense of how old I am, since public school prayer stopped in 1962), and I'm sure I was not the only child who thought "Harold" was God's name and that we prayed not to be led into Penn Station.

That we do not address God by a personal name does not prevent an intimate relationship, for in the biblical tradition God is "father" as well as "king," "friend" and also "savior." When we use English words like *God* or *Lord*, we should take the time to think of the sacredness of the address and the amazing, truly amazing fact that despite divine holiness, we have this intimate connection.

Mary makes the connection explicit: "He shows mercy to everyone, from one generation to the next" (1:50). Mary recognizes God's

fidelity in the past and present, and so knows, in her spirit and soul, that this covenantal fidelity continues to the future. Paul makes the same point in Romans 11:29, "God's gifts and calling can't be taken back."

The next verses show how this mercy is manifested. Although we may not think that God "has scattered those with arrogant thoughts and proud inclinations," "pulled the powerful down from their thrones," or "filled the hungry with good things" (1:51, 52, 53). Mary speaks as if these reversals of fortune had already happened. She is singing the same song Hannah sang, a thousand years earlier, "God raises the poor from the dust, / lifts up the needy from the garbage pile" (1 Samuel 2:8). We see the accomplishment of these reversals in the songs of Hannah and Mary, in their lives, and in the lives of their children. We see the accomplishment whenever those who have give to those who need. We see it in servant-leadership, and we see it in fidelity to Torah and later to Gospel. We see these miracles because, as God's children, it is our responsibility to carry them out.

This is not a gospel of gain; this is a gospel of trust. It's not a gospel of wealth; it's a gospel of thanks. Mary ends her prayer with a remembrance, a recollection, of God's servant Israel, of God's promises of mercy, of God's promise to Abraham and his descendants. The new covenant that Jesus offers, in his body and blood, does not replace the old covenants with Abraham or Moses or David. It rather is a continuation of them. Those ancient promises have a universal import, for God had promised Abraham, "I will make of you a great nation and will bless you. I will make your name respected, and you will be a blessing. I will bless those who bless you, those who curse you I will curse; all the families of the earth will be blessed because of you" (Genesis 12:2-3). From one people, faithful to the Torah, come the messages, "You must love your neighbor as yourself," and "Any

immigrant who lives with you must be treated as if they were one of your citizens" (Leviticus 19:18, 34). When these commandments are kept, by all who hold the text as sacred, the hungry are fed.

Mary stayed with Elizabeth for about three months and then returned to her home. Since Elizabeth was six months pregnant when Mary arrived, Luke tells us Mary left right before John's birth. Although Luke does not explain why Mary left, I think she left out of graciousness. She thought, "This is the time for Elizabeth and Zechariah to rejoice. The time will come for the world to rejoice in my child, but not yet."

Chapter 3

THE JOURNEY TO JOY

Chapter 3

THE JOURNEY TO JOY

In those days Caesar Augustus declared that everyone throughout the empire should be enrolled in the tax lists. This first enrollment occurred when Quirinius governed Syria. Everyone went to their own cities to be enrolled. Since Joseph belonged to David's house and family line, he went up from the city of Nazareth in Galilee to David's city, called Bethlehem, in Judea. He went to be enrolled together with Mary, who was promised to him in marriage and who was pregnant. While they were there, the time came for Mary to have her baby. She gave birth to her firstborn child, a son, wrapped him snugly, and laid him in a manger, because there was no place for them in the guestroom.

Nearby shepherds were living in the fields, guarding their sheep at night. The Lord's angel stood before them, the Lord's glory shone around them, and they were terrified.

The angel said, "Don't be afraid! Look! I bring good news to you—wonderful, joyous news for all people. Your savior is born today in David's city. He is Christ the Lord. This is a sign for you: you will find a newborn baby wrapped snugly and lying in a manger." Suddenly a great assembly of the

*heavenly forces was with the angel praising God. They said,
"Glory to God in heaven, and on earth peace among those
whom he favors."*

*When the angels returned to heaven, the shepherds said to
each other, "Let's go right now to Bethlehem and see what's
happened. Let's confirm what the Lord has revealed to us."
They went quickly and found Mary and Joseph, and the
baby lying in the manger. When they saw this, they reported
what they had been told about this child. Everyone who
heard it was amazed at what the shepherds told them. Mary
committed these things to memory and considered them
carefully. The shepherds returned home, glorifying and
praising God for all they had heard and seen. Everything
happened just as they had been told.*

*When eight days had passed, Jesus' parents circumcised him
and gave him the name Jesus. This was the name given to
him by the angel before he was conceived. When the time
came for their ritual cleansing, in accordance with the Law
from Moses, they brought Jesus up to Jerusalem to present
him to the Lord. (It's written in the Law of the Lord, "Every
firstborn male will be dedicated to the Lord.") They offered a
sacrifice in keeping with what's stated in the Law of the Lord,
A pair of turtledoves or two young pigeons.*

*A man named Simeon was in Jerusalem. He was righteous
and devout. He eagerly anticipated the restoration of Israel,
and the Holy Spirit rested on him. The Holy Spirit revealed
to him that he wouldn't die before he had seen the Lord's
Christ. Led by the Spirit, he went into the temple area.
Meanwhile, Jesus' parents brought the child to the temple
so that they could do what was customary under the Law.
Simeon took Jesus in his arms and praised God. He said,*

"Now, master, let your servant go in peace according to
your word,

> *because my eyes have seen your salvation.*
> *You prepared this salvation in the presence of all peoples.*
> *It's a light for revelation to the Gentiles*
> *and a glory for your people Israel."*

His father and mother were amazed by what was said about
him. Simeon blessed them and said to Mary his mother,
"This boy is assigned to be the cause of the falling and rising
of many in Israel and to be a sign that generates opposition
so that the inner thoughts of many will be revealed. And a
sword will pierce your innermost being too."

There was also a prophet, Anna the daughter of Phanuel,
who belonged to the tribe of Asher. She was very old. After
she married, she lived with her husband for seven years. She
was now an 84-year-old widow. She never left the temple
area but worshipped God with fasting and prayer night and
day. She approached at that very moment and began to praise
God and to speak about Jesus to everyone who was looking
forward to the redemption of Jerusalem.

When Mary and Joseph had completed everything required
by the Law of the Lord, they returned to their hometown,
Nazareth in Galilee. The child grew up and became strong.
He was filled with wisdom, and God's favor was on him.

Luke 2:1-40

The birth of John the Baptist is set in the hill country of Judea
during the reign of King Herod. John's conception, birth, and circumcision take place on the national stage, and his work will be primarily
with his fellow Jews. The story of Jesus begins, as does that of John,
locally in Israel, in "Nazareth, a city in Galilee" (Luke 1:26), but his

birth in the context of the Roman census signals an empire-wide focus. John's message will be for his fellow Jews; Jesus' message is not just for the people and land of Israel, but for the "all the world."

The Census

Luke emphasizes this universal focus: "In those days a decree went out from Emperor Augustus that all the world should be registered" (2:1 NRSV). The Greek word underlying "decree" is *dogma*. Caesar issued a ruling; to resist would mean war and death.

Luke's concern is more theological than historical, for there was no empire-wide census under Augustus. Nor did Rome take a census when there was a local king on the throne, for the census would have been the task of the local monarch. At the time of Jesus' birth, there was a local king, Herod the Great. We might think of the census as a parable more than a possibility, and as a parable, the tale it tells is profound.

We gain additional insight into Luke's pastoral purpose when we consider what a census is intended to do. Today, a census determines the need for political representation and for social services. Not so in the ancient world: then, a census determined the local tax base as well as, in some cases, the number of men who could be conscripted for military service. We see here the power of Rome, power based on monarch, money, and the military. And we also know Luke is providing an alternative, the kingdom of God based on care of the poor, servant-leadership, and treasures in heaven.

Luke tells us that "everyone went to their own cities to be enrolled" (2:3), which was also not the case historically. Given the mobile population of the first century, returning to one's hometown to be enrolled would have created a logistical nightmare. One registered where one lived. Luke's description is thus both symbolic

and practical: the census provides the Evangelist one more occasion to indicate Joseph's Davidic connection, and it also helps explain why "Jesus of Nazareth" was born not in Nazareth in Galilee. Luke tells us, "Joseph belonged to David's house and family line, [and] he went up from the city of Nazareth in Galilee to David's city, called Bethlehem, in Judea. He went to be enrolled together with Mary, who was promised to him in marriage and who was pregnant" (2:4-5). Here we see more of the fulfillment of Gabriel's promises to Mary.

Matthew, who locates Mary and Joseph already in Judea, does not mention a census; Matthew does not need to do so because Matthew has a different story, with equally important elements, to present. In Matthew's Gospel, Mary, Joseph, and the baby move from Judea to Egypt to Galilee as Matthew presents Jesus as a new Moses. Luke suggests that the followers of Jesus will be on the move, from their place of birth to the ends of the earth.

Luke's concern is also more ethical than it is historical, as we see from the next two verses: "This first enrollment occurred when Quirinius governed Syria. Everyone went to their own cities to be enrolled" (2:2-3). Quirinius, whom we know from Roman records, was not the legate while Herod the Great ruled. Herod died in 4 BCE, and Quirinius received his appointment in 6 CE. The reference to Quirinius is therefore not a historical factoid; it is designed to remind readers about political leaders who promote armed rebellion. Again, we need to know the historical context.

In the year 6 CE, after the death of Herod the Great and when Jesus would have been a child, Rome proclaimed a local census. At this time, a Galilean known as "Judas the Galilean" (here, as with all the Marys, we have a combined problem of lack of last names coupled with too many people named Judas) began a revolt. We know that Luke knows about Judas because Judas appears in Gamaliel's speech in Acts 5:37: "At the time of the census, Judas the Galilean

appeared and got some people to follow him in a revolt. He was killed too, and all his followers scattered far and wide."

Now, in light of Acts, we see why Luke so subtly speaks of the census. Luke's readers know that Jesus is from Nazareth in Galilee, and they know that Jesus proclaimed the "kingdom of God," which does sound political. By setting Jesus' birth in the context of a census, Luke announces that Jesus and his followers are *not* part of a movement intent on military revolt. Instead of rebelling, Mary and Joseph obey the governmental command, no matter the personal hardship.

The Birth of Jesus

The "room in the inn" today generally connotes homeless shelters or church-based programs for those in need. Behind such institutions is often the sense that Mary and Joseph, a poor peasant couple, were turned away from the local hotel because they lacked sufficient funds. The message may be a helpful prompt for today's social services, but it is not based in any history. When some modern versions of the story include a nasty hotel owner, or innkeeper, cast as the "greedy Jew," biblical story descends into nasty stereotyping.

I recently heard the explanation that the inn-keeper was concerned that Mary, by giving birth, would render the room ritually impure, and that's why he evicted them from public space and banished them to the barn. This is also nonsense. Most people are impure most of the time and most don't care. There was no sign outside the inn reading, "no menstruating women, no men who have recently ejaculated, no women who have recently given birth, and no one who has within the past week attended a funeral permitted." The scene has nothing to do with either poverty or purity.

Luke simply states, "And she gave birth to her firstborn son and wrapped him in bands of cloth, and laid him in a manger, because

there was no place for them in the inn" (Luke 2:7 NRSV). The point is that there is no room—that is, no place for them at the inn—for Mary *to give birth*. Inns were public spaces; Mary needed privacy.

More, the stable allows Luke to make a profound point that many readers today miss because we don't think about the metaphoric potential of words. The term *manger* is not just a bed of straw; it is a feeding trough. Those who remember their high-school French should recall the verb *manger*, "to eat." Mary places her baby where food is found; how appropriate, for this baby will later take "the bread . . . saying, 'This is my body, which is given for you. Do this in remembrance of me'" (22:19). By locating Jesus in the manger, Luke is anticipating the Communion story. More, the name *Bethlehem* literally means "house of bread." If you go to a traditional Jewish household or a service where there's a meal, you would begin with the grace before meals: "Blessed are you, Lord our God, ruler of the universe, *ha motzi lechem min ha'aretz*, who brings forth bread (*lechem*) from the earth." We should remember the manger in Bethlehem not only at the Last Supper but also in connection to all the passages where Jesus shares a meal with others. Luke depicts the feeding of the five thousand, meals with tax collectors and sinners including Zacchaeus, the three meals with Pharisees, the dinner at Emmaus, and the final meal of broiled fish. Reading Luke should make one hungry, not just for bread, but for more of the story.

Even the bands of cloth—or the CEB's "wrapped snugly" or the KJV's "swaddling clothes" (Luke 2:7)—have a biblical connection, but for this we need to go to the Catholic, Anglican, and Orthodox canons. According to Wisdom of Solomon 7:4-6, King Solomon is "nurtured by snug clothes and good care. No king has ever begun life any differently. There's only one way into life for everyone, and only one way out as well." Jesus, fully human, enters the world as do all other babies. Fully human, he will die as do all other people.

Finally, the reference to a "firstborn" son also suggests, at least for some readers, that Mary and Joseph had sexual relations following Jesus' birth. That is because firstborn presumes there are others. *Firstborn child* is usually seen as a different designation than *only child*. On a surface reading, the New Testament suggests that Mary had other children. Matthew 13:55 (see Mark 6:3) questions, "Isn't he the carpenter's son? Isn't his mother named Mary? Aren't James, Joseph, Simon, and Judas his brothers?" In Mark, by the way, Jesus himself is the carpenter. According to Matthew 13:55, he is said to be the son of a carpenter. Whether Mary and Joseph had children after Jesus depends upon one's personal view. For some traditions, as we see already with the *Protevangelium*, Mary remained a virgin perpetually, and, in later accounts, even Joseph was a virgin. In other traditions, Mary and Joseph had a normal relationship, as married couples do, after the birth of Jesus.

I do not have the gift of celibacy (granted, this might be too much information; then again, I have a husband of more than three decades and two children), but I have friends, women and men, who do, and who have dedicated their lives to helping others. In our sexually saturated society, I find Mary's virginity a refreshing move of independence.

The Shepherds

The scene shifts from the inn to the outdoors, where "nearby shepherds were living in the fields, guarding their sheep at night" (Luke 2:8). This is not wintertime, for at night both sheep and shepherd would freeze. It is to these shepherds that an angel, again, appears. First to Zechariah in the Temple in Jerusalem, then to Mary in her home in Nazareth of Galilee, then back to Judea in the fields outside of Bethlehem. The divine messenger can be anywhere, and so therefore can the message: from religious institution, to home, to field.

At this point, a number of ill-informed commentators rush in to explain how these shepherds represent ritual impurity, and so they conclude that Jesus does not care about and therefore does away with purity laws. Nonsense. Shepherds are no more and no less ritually impure than anyone else. We might even imagine that the flocks over which they keep watch are the flocks that will be dedicated for Temple sacrifice.

For Luke, the shepherds have nothing to do with purity, but they do have symbolic value. First, they provide, as do Mary and Joseph, a contrast to Caesar Augustus. They are in the field where they protect their animals: they represent those who care for the vulnerable. They may also remind us of other shepherds: Rebecca, Rachel, Moses, and David. And we will remember them when Jesus, not in Luke's Gospel but in Matthew, Mark, and John, speaks of himself as the shepherd of his people.

We can picture these shepherds, under the stars. They are doing what people do at the end of the day: telling stories, singing songs, praying to God for good health or for the Romans to go away, talking about household troubles or joys. Perhaps there are women among the shepherds, gathered together to tell their own stories and to share their own dreams.

It is to these shepherds that the angel appears with his now-expected "don't be afraid" (2:10). I can imagine a house church in antiquity, where a visiting disciple is performing the Gospel of Luke. As soon as the angel appears and before the disciple can get to the line, the members of the assembly call out as one, "Do not fear!"

The angel then offers "good news to you—wonderful, joyous news for all people" (2:10). The reference to "good news" is the term *euangelion* in Greek. Whereas in Mark (1:1) and Matthew (4:23), the term primarily relates to Jesus' mission, for Luke the good news begins with his birth. We've already seen that euangelion means

Salvation means that there is respite from whatever oppresses in the community that hears, and lives, this Gospel. Men and women, slaves and free people, all come together to say, "In our midst, we have a savior."

"good news" and how it usually had secular, political implications. Luke's readers—and readers of this guide—know of the Decree that proclaimed the birthday of the "god" Augustus Caesar. We readers also know that this new "good news" does not come from the seat of earthly power but from heaven above. When the Gospel speaks about "good news," the content has to be more than "you will have eternal life." To jump to the Cross without attending to the good news of John, and then of the birth of Jesus, is to miss the "gospel" in all senses of the term. Luke takes this secular term and nuances it: what good news will this new king, heir of David and Son of God, bring? To find the answer, we must continue to read through Luke's "Gospel," Luke's "good news."

For the shepherds, the immediate good news is universal: it is "joyous" for "all people" (2:10). Here's a contrast to the census, which was one of displacement, if not worse, for all the world. The shepherds learn that a savior has been born in the city of David. The universal is always anchored in the particular: Jesus is fully located in Jewish geography and Jewish lineage because, as Mary sang (1:55), he is the fulfillment of the promises to Israel.

What kind of a savior he is will need to be shown. The texts that will become the Old Testament typically speak of salvation as an event that occurs in history, as in being saved from war, hunger, disease, plague, and oppression. For people in Luke's church, salvation comes to mean salvation from sin and death. But it must also keep that original focus on the desperate needs of people in our own time. Salvation means that there is respite from whatever oppresses in the community that hears, and lives, this Gospel. Men and women, slaves and free people, all come together to say, "In our midst, we have a savior." For Jesus to be a savior and for the good news to function as salvific, the Gospel says that we do not need to wait until some far-flung future. We can see salvation in the actions

of the past, as at the Exodus, where Miriam and Moses insisted on freedom. We can see it in the present, as Luke's parable of the good Samaritan demonstrates. And we can anticipate it tomorrow, if we simply follow John the Baptist's instruction: share what you have with those in need (3:11).

The sign the shepherds receive is not a supernova or even the angel (which should have been sign enough). It is those bands of cloth, the manger, and the baby. The refusal to offer signs of supernatural status fits within Luke's infancy stories. The sign to Mary was the pregnancy of her cousin Elizabeth. Once we figure out the sign, whether of a pregnant woman, of a mother who has just given birth, of a newborn, even of baby clothes or a stable, our next step is to work out the symbolism, or what that sign "signifies." If we can start to look for the light of the divine in front of our eyes rather than search the stars, we'll be ready when we hear stories of sowers and seeds, vines and fig trees, yeast and fish. Signs are all around us, if we take the time to look.

The celestial choir that appears to the shepherds is usually called the "heavenly host"; the CEB offers "heavenly forces" (2:13), which is the better translation for today. This is God's army. No wonder they can sing about "peace among those whom he favors" (2:14); they are the peace-keeping force of the universe. When I was little, I was familiar with the expression "Lord of Hosts," and I thought that the "Lord of Hosts" was someone who invited you to a beautiful home for dinner, found you a place at the table, and did not make you drink the icky tomato juice if you did not want to. I had no clue that the hosts were warrior angels. I still think I like my explanation better. I prefer the Lord of Hosts who presides over a meal rather than over the military.

The shepherds decide to go to Bethlehem to "see what's happened" (2:15). The angels do not go with them. Angels continue

to appear in Luke, but in pronouncements rather than in person. The next appearance, in a verse that does not appear in many early copies of Luke, occurs when Jesus, on the Mount of Olives, prays, "take this cup of suffering away from me" (22:42). We read, "Then a heavenly angel appeared to him and strengthened him" (22:43). But here in the early part of the Gospel, the focus is on joy.

The shepherds don't see a baby that glows in the dark, or one fully verbal, or even one with a complete set of teeth. They see the baby, snuggled in his wrappings. There is nothing particularly special about what their eyes see; there is everything special about how they interpret what they see.

When we see the shepherds, we see Luke express another concern. Jesus himself needs angels less than he needs these people. He wants the human companionship, and he wants humanity to be more like companions, able fully to love their neighbors. I also suspect that Mary and Joseph appreciated more the shepherds' visit than another angelic annunciation, with all the "do not fear" and "here's what else will rock your world." It's overwhelming enough to have a baby, especially if you're far from home. It's even more overwhelming when the heavenly host shows up in the stable. Luke tells us: pay attention to earthly matters, neighbors and relatives, shepherds, and who else might be at the inn. Celestial armies can wait.

Luke tells us that the shepherds saw not just the baby but also "Mary and Joseph" (2:16). For all the wonder of Gabriel's annunciation to Mary and all the celebration of the Magnificat, we see Mary and Joseph as they are: tired, joyful at having arrived safely in Bethlehem, relieved to find a private place for giving birth.

The shepherds report to Mary and Joseph what the angel said about the baby. I can picture Mary, having had her own conversation with an angel, nodding along. Luke tells us that she "committed these things to memory and considered them carefully" (2:19). The signs

will gradually unfold, not only to be treasured but also to be more fully understood as time passes. Like photographs (at least before we all started snapping pictures on our phones), the Gospel stories develop over time. Each subsequent report in Luke, each reference to an angel, to a meal, to a promise, will give new meaning to the Christmas events.

Moreover, the visit of the shepherds, like Mary's visit to Elizabeth, transforms all the parties involved. The shepherds function as a "sign" to Mary; they assure her, "yes, what you experienced was not a hallucination; yes, no matter how unbelievable everything has been, believe!"

At the same time, by explicitly mentioning Joseph, Luke assures us that he, too, has confirmation of whatever Mary had told him. Sometimes we are more willing to hear the truth from outsiders than to believe it ourselves. The doctor's two-sentence pronouncement about diet or health can have more impact than a spouse's twenty-year insistence.

Today we see the shepherds in every manger scene; the "three kings" are there too, but the Magi are only in Matthew, and Matthew has no manger scene. I suspect most people remember the statues of the Magi more vividly than they do the shepherds; the Magi have fancier clothes, most distinguishable features, better gifts. Luke keeps the eye on one message of the Gospel: the lifting up of the lowly. Matthew offers other concerns: the response of the gentile nations to this Jewish king and, from Herod's reaction to the Magi's announcement of his birth, the clash between earthly and heavenly kingdoms. Luke tells the story through Mary's experience; Matthew concentrates on Joseph. The gospel takes different forms that will speak to us with different messages at different times.

Perhaps Joseph, here in Luke's account, was thinking, "I hope they read the story of my own angelic dreams," but for that, we have

to wait for chapter 4. As the shepherds go off to tell about what they had seen and heard, thus becoming some of the earliest "evangelists," Luke turns attention to Jesus' heritage in Israel.

Marking Jewish Identity

Jewish identity, from antiquity to the present, is marked on the male body by circumcision. Luke has already recounted John's circumcision and naming; in 2:21, we see these rituals again. Whereas Elizabeth had to convince everyone that her child should be named "John," there is no debate over Jesus' name. Early listeners to the Gospel of Luke would remember the angel's conversation with Mary and her response; they would not have had to wait for another Sunday morning to hear another part of the lectionary. We can, and should, savor each event individually, but we should also appreciate them as connected into a larger whole. We cannot fully understand the Annunciation until we have witnessed the birth; we cannot fully understand the birth until we have walked with Jesus from Galilee to Jerusalem, and we cannot fully understand this journey until we have gone to the cross, the tomb, Emmaus, and back to Jerusalem.

From 1568 until 1960, the Roman Catholic Church celebrated on January 1 the "Circumcision of the Lord and the Octave [eight days after, counting Christmas] of the Nativity." Eastern Orthodox as well as Byzantine-rite Catholics retain this feast on their liturgical calendars, and there is an effort in some Roman Catholic circles to have the feast reinstated. It would accompany the present designation for this day, known as the "Solemnity of Mary, Mother of God" (this term may be familiar also to people in Anglican and Lutheran traditions). Today, many churches focus not on the circumcision, but on the naming.

At the time of Jesus, and to this day, circumcision is a sign of Jewish identity. It is the sign of God's covenant with Abraham, it is

the practice for which Maccabean mothers and their infant sons were martyred, and it is Paul's evidence of his covenantal fidelity: "I was circumcised on the eighth day. I am from the people of Israel and the tribe of Benjamin. I am a Hebrew of the Hebrews" (Philippians 3:5).

This shift in emphasis from circumcision to naming, and from the sign of the covenant to the role of Mary, makes some sense given the post-World War II cultural climate: circumcision seems "too Jewish" or "too particular" or too fleshy or for some just too weird. Paul did not require it of his gentile disciples, and as gentiles became the majority in the church, circumcision became a marker of something other, of someone other.

Before we dismiss this ritual as meaningless, or worse, we should attend to what it represents for Jesus. In a single line, Luke tells us that Jesus is, like John, fully a member of the Jewish people, not just by birth, but also in the body. Because circumcision also involves blood, when we get to the Last Supper and these words, "This cup is the new covenant by my blood, which is poured out for you" (Luke 22:20), we remember this first sign of the covenant. Just as Mary talked about the promises God made to Abraham, in this single verse she and Joseph fulfill their part of the covenant with Abraham. They are faithful to the tradition, in which following Torah is not a burden but a blessing.

Luke continues to emphasize their embeddedness in Jewish tradition, and anyone familiar with ritual—baptism, confirmation, graduation, whatever formal action makes us members of a community—should be able to see the value. Ritual, when performed with full understanding, helps to anchor our identity. Although Luke's reference to "their ritual cleansing, in accordance with the Law from Moses" (2:22) is not known in Jewish sources, for the father is not considered to be in a state of impurity after a birth, Luke could be reflecting a tradition not elsewhere preserved. My own suspicion is

Ritual, when performed
with full understanding,
helps to anchor
our identity.

that Luke wants to emphasize Mary and Joseph's complete fidelity to their tradition. They are not "merely going through the rituals"; they are affirming their own and their son's identity as part of the people Israel.

When Mary and Joseph go up to Jerusalem to present their child to God, Luke offers the Gospel's first quotation from the Torah: "It's written in the Law of the Lord, 'Every firstborn male will be dedicated to the Lord'" (2:23). The citation is a paraphrase of Exodus 13:2, "Dedicate to me all your oldest children. Each first offspring from any Israelite womb belongs to me, whether human or animal" (see also Exodus 22:29-30). The original commandment in Exodus may have indicated that early in Israel's history, the priestly class was comprised of firstborn sons. Later, members of the tribe of Levi (Levites) served in priestly capacities. Still later, the descendants of Aaron, the brother of Moses, became the priests. Zechariah and Elizabeth, the parents of John the Baptist, would have had Aaron as one of their ancestors.

In Jewish practice, firstborn sons, on the thirty-first day after their birth, are "redeemed" from this dedication by a ceremony called the *pidyon ha-ben*, the "redemption of the son." The father redeems the child by making a charitable donation, traditionally of silver coins. This ritual, too, comes from the Torah. Exodus 13:13b states, "You should ransom every oldest male among your children." The scripture goes on to explain the meaning of the practice, which is related less to priesthood than to salvation: "When in the future your child asks you, 'What does this mean?' you should answer 'The Lord brought us with great power out of Egypt, out of the place we were slaves. When Pharaoh refused to let us go, the Lord killed all the oldest offspring in the land of Egypt, from the oldest sons to the oldest male animals'" (Exodus 13:14-15a). All this background is also part of the context for Luke's verse.

The Torah does not require a formal presentation of a child. It is possible that by noting a presentation, Luke is thinking of Hannah's presentation of her son, Samuel, to the temple at Shiloh. In 1 Samuel 1:28, Hannah tells Eli the priest, "So now I give this boy back to the LORD. As long as he lives, he is given to the LORD." Just as Mary, like Hannah before her, sang a song of divine redemption, so Mary will learn, as did Hannah, that she will have to let her son go. She cannot protect him forever.

Mary and Joseph then make their offering, with another citation from Torah accompanying them: "what's stated in the Law of the LORD, *A pair of turtledoves or two young pigeons*" (Luke 2:24, paraphrasing Leviticus 12:8). The sacrifice is a simple one, one that everyone could afford. The Temple system worked on what we might consider a sliding scale: people participated as they were able. Like Zechariah and Elizabeth, Joseph and Mary are "righteous before God, blameless in their observance of all the Lord's commandments and regulations" (Luke 1:6).

Luke's stress on the physical and biological—including the concerns about how an elderly couple might miraculously have a biological child, the conceptions of John and Jesus, childbirth, circumcision, and attention to purity laws as well as to rituals described in the Torah—serves to show Jesus' humanity and his role in fulfilling promises to Israel. All this detail provides a counter to a movement that had gained in popularity in the second century CE, a movement known as "Marcionism." Named after Marcion, a follower of Jesus who concluded that the God of the "Old Testament" (not a term he used, but you know what I mean) was a distinct god from the one Jesus proclaimed. Marcion was not in favor of the various commandments concerning distinct Jewish identity; he was also convinced that Creation, with all of its "fleshy" aspects, was a flawed system created by a flawed deity.

Marcionism, a heresy, is still alive and well in churches today. It surfaces every time someone makes a remark about the "Old Testament God of Law" versus the "New Testament God of grace." It also surfaces whenever people talk about how the commandments are nonsense, or worse. Luke's infancy material insists that the "Old Testament" is not to be dismissed; nor is it some dusty book to be kept on a shelf and trotted out just to see how Jesus "fulfills" certain verses. It is a book that continues to be interpreted, and it is a book that records the traditions by which Jews, from before the time of Jesus to today, identified themselves, kept themselves from being swallowed up into ancient empires, and sanctified their God. It was through interpreting these pages that Jesus and his earliest followers proclaimed their own identity, for there was no "New Testament" at the time.

Luke claims for the followers of Jesus the traditions of ancient Israel and Second Temple Judaism. As "Father Abraham" will tell the rich man in the famous parable of the rich man and Lazarus, "They have Moses and the Prophets. They must listen to them" (16:29). To understand Luke's Gospel, and to understand Jesus, we do well to know the traditions that they knew, the stories that they told, the Laws that they held sacred.

Simeon's Consolation

The infancy materials conclude when Mary and Joseph encounter, in the Temple, two elderly, righteous Jews. We first meet in Jerusalem (Luke specifies the location) Simeon, who, like his counterpart Zechariah, the father of John the Baptist whom we also first meet in Jerusalem and in the Temple, "was righteous and devout" (2:25a). The CEV's translation of "Simeon was a good man" does not capture the spirit of the text. The words *righteous* and *devout* suggest a particular connection to Israel; *good man* is generic. "You're a good

man, Charlie Brown," does not suggest prayer in the Temple or hope in the promises to Abraham.

While Zechariah was likely praying for a son, Simeon has a broader focus: he was "looking forward" to what the NRSV calls "the consolation of Israel" and what the CEB paraphrases as "eagerly [anticipating] the restoration of Israel" (2:25b). The problem here is that Luke is not using "salvation" language. The term in Greek (*parakalesis*) is not "to save" but literally "to console" or "to comfort." It is the verbal form of the Greek word *paraclete* that appears in John's Gospel to identify the Holy Spirit, translated variously as "comforter" or "advocate." Simeon wants comfort and consolation: knowing of war, he wanted peace; knowing of Roman rule and Herodian rule, he wanted divine rule.

Like Mary and Elizabeth and Zechariah, Simeon is also inspired by the Holy Spirit (2:25c); once Luke notes this point, we immediately know that a prophecy is coming. But now the revelation makes a subtle shift, from canticles of joy to notices of danger. Simeon first introduces death into the story. The Spirit had revealed to him that he would not die until "he had seen the Lord's Christ" (2:26). This is a mixed message, with some irony. He wants to see the child, because that child will bring about the consolation that he seeks; he may not want to see the child, because once he has that encounter, he will die. I think Simeon was tired, and he wanted to rest. But he would not until he, personally, could have that comfort and consolation.

Like Mary and Joseph, Simeon comes to the Temple. Mary and Joseph come to the Temple to fulfill "what was customary under the Law" (2:27)—again, Luke highlights their fidelity to Torah—while Simeon is guided by the Spirit. The two guides, Spirit and Torah, are not mutually exclusive.

Luke tells us that Simeon took Jesus in his arms (2:28); missing, but necessary, is the initial meeting between old prophet and young

parents. We can picture this elderly man, with a white beard and eyes that do not see as well as they once did, with wrinkled hands carefully touching the child. Mary hands him her baby, and the old man cradles new life. Simeon is thinking to himself, "Yes, this child is what I had been waiting for. This child, and his parents, give me the comfort to know that when I die, my people will continue." We do not know if Simeon had a wife or any children of his own. But now, this child becomes his child, the one who will answer his prayers.

Holding the baby, Simeon speaks not directly to Mary or Joseph but to God. He begins with praise and then says, "Now, master, let your servant [Greek *doulos*, literally 'slave'] go in peace according to your word" (2:29). Simeon's life is over; he has stayed watch, and now he is relieved. The old man states, "My eyes have seen your salvation" (2:30), an eloquent expression, since now he is about to close his eyes. He was seeking consolation and comfort. He has found more; he has found salvation. His prayer (2:29-32), called the *Nunc Dimittis* from the Latin for "Now you dismiss," is the affirmation of his desires. Today, it is associated with evening worship, as if everyone can say, at the end of the day, "I have been faithful and now God will let me sleep in comfort and protection."

The salvation is good news not just for Simeon, or even just for all Israel. Now Simeon brings home the implications of that census, the setting on the world stage. He proclaims that the child will be "a light of revelation to the Gentiles" (2:32a). Pagans, also seeking peace and consolation, need this good news as well. As Simeon's eyes dim, he can picture this light, growing brighter.

Because the Jewish people already have this light—as we had already seen with Zechariah and Elizabeth, Mary and Joseph—the meaning of the child to them is something different. Simeon proclaims that the child is "a glory for your people Israel" (2:32b). Speaking of

a small group of people, whose homeland is on the outskirts of the empire, whose land has come into Roman control, he reassures Mary and Joseph, and anyone listening, that the promises to Abraham will be fulfilled.

Joseph and Mary, here called the child's "father and mother"—these very human parents—are amazed by what they hear (2:33). Mary had an angelic annunciation; both parents heard the words of the shepherds. But they still remain awed. The good news requires repeating because we can, in day-to-day activities, lose sight of it. Our hopes in the fulfillment of promises fade. The shepherds have heard the promise of joy "for all people" (2:10) and the blessing "on earth peace among those whom he favors" (2:14). Now Simeon assures us of the international impact of these revelations.

Simeon then blesses the parents (2:34a). Mary had stated that "everyone will consider me highly favored" (1:48), and Simeon begins the fulfillment of this prediction. But blessing, and calling, can come at a price. Only to Mary, who is continuing to ponder the angel's message, does he state that consolation will also come with conflict. "This boy is assigned to be the cause of the falling and rising of so many in Israel" (2:34), he begins. The prediction confirms what Mary, and centuries before her, Hannah, had already proclaimed: "He has pulled the powerful down from their thrones and lifted up the lowly" (1:52). But then he adds that the child is to "be a sign that generates opposition" (2:34c).

In terms of messianic ideas, the opposition from many Jews to the claims of Jesus' status should not be a surprise. The dominant Jewish idea at the time (and subsequently) is that the Messiah brings about the messianic age, a time when death no longer has dominion, when there is a general resurrection of the dead, a final judgment, the return of exiles to their homeland, peace on earth. Because Jesus did not bring about this type of salvation, most Jews concluded that

The best way of evangelizing is not to tell the potential convert, "Here's what's wrong with your tradition." The best way to evangelize is to show that potential convert, "Here's what's right with my tradition; here's how it prompts toward action; here's how it consoles."

he could not be the Messiah. What Christians sometimes describe as the "Second Coming" looks, to a great extent, like traditional Jewish messianic hopes. The only difference is the identity of the Messiah, who in Jewish tradition is not a divine being to be worshiped, but a representative of the one God.

Rather than having us engage in endless (or, at least until the end of the world) speculation about messianic job descriptions, it makes more sense to me to work together for justice and peace, and let God take care of the end-of-the-world details.

Many gentiles, here the pagan nations, will also oppose Jesus and his messengers. They have their own gods and their own traditions, and they do not want to be told by missionaries that their theologies and practices are evil or corrupt or stupid. They have a point. The best way of evangelizing is not to tell the potential convert, "Here's what's wrong with your tradition." The best way to evangelize is to show that potential convert, "Here's what's right with my tradition; here's how it prompts toward action; here's how it consoles."

There will also be opposition to Jesus from among his own followers. Judas will betray him; Peter will deny him. Others, such as Marcion, may deform the original good news or use it for political and economic gain rather than to create love of neighbor and stranger. Sometimes the opposition is of a more personal concern. When Jesus speaks of taking up the cross, the response may be, "It's too hard," or, "It's too dangerous." In such cases, Simeon assures us that God knows what we are thinking: "the inner thoughts of many will be revealed" (2:35a). That revelation, for all to see, is found in the fruit that people bear, good and bad.

Finally, Simeon, still holding the child, tells Mary that "a sword will pierce your innermost being too" (2:35b). The Greek literally says, "A sword will pierce your own soul [*psyche*]." Jesus is not the only one who will suffer; his mother, letting her son go from her

and to his death, will suffer as well. That comment reminds me of John 19:34: "One of the soldiers pierced his side with a spear, and immediately blood and water came out." This description, only in the Gospel of John, hints at Jesus, metaphorically, giving new birth to his followers; it is through the gift of his body that they can be, as he tells Nicodemus, "born anew" or "born from above" (John 3:3, 7 CEB, NRSV). When Jesus dies, John tells us that his mother is at the foot of the cross. And there, she feels the sword and the life draining from her as well.

But like that of her son, her story does not end here. The pain of losing her child remains, but the hope for consolation and restoration remains as well.

Simeon, his hopes fulfilled, is now ready to let go. He has the comfort he needs. And he will not be alone.

Anna the Prophet

Luke then tells us that Mary was not the only woman in the Temple to hear Simeon's words. We now meet Anna, called "a prophet" like Miriam and Deborah and Huldah before her. Her name recollects Hannah of 1 Samuel, and it anticipates St. Anne, Mary's mother according to postbiblical texts. We do not know Mary's background, but we know that Joseph is a descendant of King David. Now the situation is reversed: Luke does not mention Simeon's background or marital status, but Anna's ancestry and marriage receive full details. She is the daughter of Phanuel (otherwise unknown, but known to her) of the tribe of Asher (Luke 2:36a).

For Luke, Anna represents the ancient lost tribes of Israel, separated from their Judean counterparts when the Assyrians destroyed the Northern Kingdom seven hundred years earlier. One major Jewish messianic image is that all twelve tribes will be reunited. That is in part why Jesus calls twelve apostles, for he is

symbolically reconstituting the twelve tribes. With Anna, Luke tells us that these tribes are still alive to history. More, Anna is from the tribe of Asher, whose name means "happy." According to Genesis 30:13, Leah, rejoicing in giving birth to another son, proclaims, "'I'm happy now because women call me happy.' So she named him Asher." Echoes of this verse now ripple through all the infancy materials: the joy of pregnancy, the recognition and rejoicing of others, attention to women's prophetic voices.

Yet unlike Mary and Elizabeth, Anna has no child: "She was very old. After she married, she lived with her husband for seven years. She was now an 84-year-old widow" (Luke 2:36b-37). The only child she needs is the one protected in Simeon's arms.

Unlike Simeon, who is brought to the Temple under the guidance of the Holy Spirit, Anna was already there: "She never left the temple area but worshiped God with fasting and prayer night and day" (2:37). For those who (incorrectly) think of the Temple as male-only space, this verse should provide correction. I like to think of Anna as a mother of the Temple, just as the childless Deborah was a mother in Israel. Her presence could be counted upon; her words had authority; her actions conveyed her righteousness. She also reminds me of that tenacious parable in Luke's parable of the widow and the judge (18: 1-8), which Luke insists is about praying always and not losing heart.

We hear Simeon's words, but we do not hear Anna's. Others, however, do, for she "began to praise God and to speak about Jesus to everyone who was looking forward to the redemption of Jerusalem" (2:38). She is like the shepherds who told others about what they had experienced. She anticipates other women who will proclaim the gospel to any who will listen. Her focus is on concerns shared to this day, for those of us who still pray for the peace of Jerusalem.

Luke does not tell us what happens to Anna and Simeon. Like Zechariah and Elizabeth, they open the story, and we can only use

our imagination to determine how they would react to the events that will follow. But we remember them, their righteousness, their hope, and their prophecies.

Ending and Beginning

Luke ends the infancy story with a charming vignette. Mary and Joseph, having completed everything required by the Law of the Lord (Luke is not going to let the Torah go!), return to their hometown, Nazareth in Galilee. They had been in Judea because of the census, and they had stayed in Judea through to the child's dedication. Jesus grows up, becomes strong, and is marked by wisdom and divine favor.

But he is also being raised by Mary and Joseph, themselves strengthened by the Spirit and by what they have heard, from angels and shepherds, and from Elizabeth and Simeon and Anna. They will have to let their son be what he is called to be, but not yet. Not yet.

Chapter 4

THE GIFTS OF THE GENTILES

Chapter 4

THE GIFTS OF THE GENTILES

This is how the birth of Jesus Christ took place. When Mary his mother was engaged to Joseph, before they were married, she became pregnant by the Holy Spirit. Joseph her husband was a righteous man. Because he didn't want to humiliate her, he decided to call off their engagement quietly. As he was thinking about this, an angel from the Lord appeared to him in a dream and said, "Joseph son of David, don't be afraid to take Mary as your wife, because the child she carries was conceived by the Holy Spirit. She will give birth to a son, and you will call him Jesus, because he will save his people from their sins." Now all of this took place so that what the Lord had spoken through the prophet would be fulfilled:

> *Look! A virgin will become pregnant and give birth to a son,*
>> *And they will call him, Emmanuel.*

(Emmanuel means "God with us.")

When Joseph woke up, he did just as an angel from God commanded and took Mary as his wife. But he didn't have sexual relations with her until she gave birth to a son. Joseph called him Jesus.

After Jesus was born in Bethlehem in the territory of Judea during the rule of King Herod, magi came from the east to Jerusalem. They asked, "Where is the newborn king of the Jews? We've seen his star in the east, and we've come to honor him."

When King Herod heard this, he was troubled, and everyone in Jerusalem was troubled with him. He gathered all the chief priests and the legal experts and asked them where the Christ was to be born. They said, "In Bethlehem of Judea, for this is what the prophet wrote:

> *You, Bethlehem, land of Judah,*
>> *by no means are you least among the rulers of Judah,*
>>> *because from you will come one who governs, who will shepherd my people Israel."*

Then Herod secretly called for the magi and found out from them the time when the star had first appeared. He sent them to Bethlehem, saying, "Go and search carefully for the child. When you've found him, report to me so that I too may go and honor him." When they heard the king, they went; and look, the star they had seen in the east went ahead of them until it stood over the place where the child was. When they saw the star, they were filled with joy. They entered the house and saw the child with Mary his mother. Falling to their knees, they honored him. Then they opened their treasure chests and presented him with gifts of gold, frankincense, and myrrh. Because they were warned in a dream not to return to Herod, they went back to their own country by another route.

When the magi had departed, an angel from the Lord appeared to Joseph in a dream and said, "Get up. Take the child and his mother and escape to Egypt. Stay there until I

*tell you, for Herod will soon search for the child in order to
kill him." Joseph got up and, during the night, took the child
and his mother to Egypt. He stayed there until Herod died.
This fulfilled what the Lord had spoken through the prophet:
I have called my son out of Egypt.*

Matthew 1:18–2:15

The Gospels of Matthew and Luke are documents of literary
genius. Each presents the story of Jesus' birth in its own way, and
each offers a narrative that challenges, that provokes, that shocks,
and that makes the reader want to hear more. Luke introduced us
to Zechariah and Elizabeth, the parents of John the Baptist, who set
the scene for the story of Mary and Joseph. From Luke's Gospel we
learn of Mary's encounter with the angel Gabriel and her visit to her
cousin Elizabeth. We hear her famous Magnificat, and we hear as
well, from Simeon, about how Jesus' mission will also pierce Mary's
own soul. Luke gives us the well-known story of the census ordered
by the Roman emperor Augustus, the travel of Mary and Joseph from
Nazareth to Bethlehem, the birth in the stable, the angelic choir, and
the shepherd's visit. Luke's infancy account ends with the prophecies
of Simeon and Anna and the return of the family to their home in
Nazareth.

Matthew has none of this! Matthew, instead of focusing on
Mary, tells the story from Joseph's perspective. Instead of shepherds,
Matthew presents the Magi, who, despite "we three kings of Orient
are," are not necessarily three, not necessarily all men, certainly not
kings, and most certainly not wise. Instead of an account of a census
that brings Mary and Joseph to Bethlehem, Matthew begins in their
home in Bethlehem and then recounts their flight to Egypt. Only after
they learn that King Herod, who sought to kill Jesus, the rival "King of
the Jews," had died, do they return to the land of Israel; however, they
relocate from Bethlehem in Judea to Nazareth in Galilee, for fear of

Herod's son Archelaus, who ruled Judea. Luke stresses Jesus' role as heir of David, and while Matthew makes this point several times as well, Matthew also depicts Jesus as a new Moses. While Luke emphasizes that all the figures in the infancy accounts were faithful to the Torah and the Prophets, Matthew makes the same point in a different way: by quoting Torah and Prophets, over and over again, to show Jesus' continuity with them.

Biblical scholars sometimes delight in pointing out discrepancies between Matthew and Luke, as if a different version of a story calls the entire tradition into question. That is a nasty move and one not warranted by the Gospels. Luke has already told us that other versions of the story of Jesus exist (1:1-4). Of course, there is more than one version, for each Evangelist has different concerns to be shared with readers. Our role as historians is to ask, "What would these stories have conveyed to the people who first heard them?" Our role as readers is also to ask, "What do these stories mean to me, and what have they meant to my community and to my tradition over time and across the globe?"

I increasingly suspect that Luke knew Matthew's story; thus, Luke's version can be seen as a supplement rather than a correction. Each Gospel narrative should be savored independently. Let's at least for a little while keep the Magi and the shepherds separate, and let's recognize that a story this magnificent should not, and cannot, be presented in only one version.

The Genealogy According to Matthew

Genealogies, generally, are interesting only to the people whose "genes" are represented. Even with Jesus, many readers race through the first seventeen verses of Matthew's Gospel, *the opening verses of the New Testament*, in order to get to verse 18, "This is how the birth of Jesus Christ took place."

I admit that I am anxious to get there too, because it is such a good story. But to pass over the genealogy is to pass up several of Matthew's major concerns. We should at least take the time to mention a few, since these notes will help us appreciate not only the story of the "birth of Jesus Christ" but also his life and his legacy. Four stops at the genealogy (we could do more) should suffice.

First, Jesus' genealogy in Luke begins at 3:23, following the story of John the Baptist's mission, and so falls out of the infancy materials. Luke also offers a reverse genealogy by beginning with Jesus and working backwards to "son of Adam son of God" (the listing also indicates that because Adam is a "son of God," all children are sons and daughters of God).

Matthew's genealogy, which opens the Gospel, starts with "Jesus Christ, son of David, son of Abraham" (1:1). Matthew will continue to stress Jesus' embeddedness in Jewish tradition: Jesus as son of David inherits the throne of David; Jesus as son of Abraham continues the promise made to the ancient patriarch. And Jesus "the Messiah" (Greek: *christos*) will preserve the ancient traditions, even as he offers his own interpretations of them.

From the opening verse to the repetition of Joseph's Davidic descent, Matthew emphasizes that Jesus is a new King David. This emphasis on David shows up not only explicitly but also by hints about David's story. For example, only in Matthew's Gospel do we learn that Judas hanged himself (in Acts 1:18, he falls headlong and dies in a field), and this death reminds us of the death of David's betrayer, Ahithophel; once he realized his plot against the king would not work, he hanged himself. According to Matthew, in order to understand Jesus, we must also understand King David. The Evangelist reinforces the connection between David and this Son of David when Jesus, dying on the cross, cites the opening verse of Psalm 22, a "psalm of David," "My God! My God, why have you left

me all alone?" We know from David's story, and from Jesus', that the lament is answered, that God keeps God's promises.

Second, Matthew's genealogy mentions four women before introducing Mary as Joseph's betrothed. Women are not completely uncommon in Israelite genealogies; to the contrary, the longest genealogy in the earlier Scriptures belongs to Judith. But the women Matthew mentions are not the expected matriarchs, Sarah, Rebecca, Leah, and Rachel. The first woman mentioned in the New Testament is Tamar, Judah's twice-widowed daughter-in-law (not to be confused with Absalom's sister Tamar); she arranges for Judah to think she is a prostitute and with him conceives twins. When Judah accuses her of committing adultery, she responds by displaying his "payment" to her: his signet, cord, and staff. Judah then proclaims her "more righteous than I am" (Genesis 38:26). She had to take action when Judah refused to marry her to his youngest son. Her action could be looked at as morally suspect, but she was in the right.

The second woman mentioned is Rahab, the prostitute from Jericho who protects the Israelite spies whom Joshua sends to do reconnaissance work in Canaan (Joshua 2; 6). Again, a woman remains faithful while the spies' motive for entering her brothel is likely not for scouting munitions. Rahab takes action when the spies do not. The third woman is Ruth, the Moabite widow who tells her mother-in-law, Naomi, "Wherever you go, I will go." Ruth, a descendant of a people conceived in incest (according to Genesis 19), chastely seduces the Bethlehemite Boaz on the threshing floor. By the next chapter, Ruth is Boaz's wife and the great-grandmother of King David. Finally, Matthew's Greek text mentions "she of Uriah," or colloquially, "the wife of Uriah." The notice is to Bathsheba, although at the time King Solomon is conceived, Bathsheba was David's wife, for David had arranged Uriah's death. It is not King David but Uriah, in 2 Samuel 11, who is the faithful one.

Much can be said about these women. Matthew appears to be making at least four points. First, women, too, contribute to salvation history, so pay attention to the women, from the genealogy to Mary the mother of Jesus to Peter's mother-in-law to the woman suffering hemorrhages to the women at the feeding of the 5,000 (the women together with the children would have pushed the attendance rate to 25,000) to that tenacious Canaanite mother and her demon-possessed daughter to the women at the cross and the tomb, and others. The story cannot proceed without them.

Second, all four women in the genealogy are involved in unexpected sexual relationships. Therefore, they anticipate Joseph's learning that his betrothed is pregnant. Matthew warns readers: do not move to snap judgments when you hear stories of adultery or prostitution; you do not know the details. All these women are "righteous" (a key term for Matthew).

Third, these women represent various family structures. Tamar was a levirate widow, who first married her dead husband's brother and only arranged her meeting with Judah when he refused to marry his youngest son to her. Rahab appears to be a single mother supporting her family. Ruth is a widow who shows loyalty to the mother of her dead husband. Bathsheba first has sexual relations with David while she is married to Uriah; when David learns she is pregnant with his child, he eventually arranges Uriah's death and then marries the pregnant widow.

Finally, Rahab is a Canaanite, Ruth is a Moabite, and Uriah, Bathsheba's first husband, is a Hittite; and all show deep loyalty to Israel and Israel's God. Similarly, Abraham himself began life as a pagan but turned to the God of Israel. Matthew tells us, through the genealogy, that the birth of Jesus will be good news not only to Jews but also to gentiles. They, too, have a part in the new movement. When Jesus encounters a Canaanite mother later (Matthew 15:21-28), we know that she, like her non-Jewish sisters in the genealogy,

will get what she wants. The penultimate verse in Matthew's Gospel is the Great Commission, "make disciples of all gentiles" (28:19, author's translation), and so the text comes full circle, for gentiles were there all the time.

Matthew's genealogy ends with a break in form: "Jacob was the father of Joseph, the husband of Mary—of whom Jesus was born, who is called the Christ" (1:16). In Luke's account, Joseph's father is named Hiel. Luke also traces the genealogy not from David and Bathsheba's son Solomon, as in Matthew's listing, but through David's son Nathan. Therefore, the two Gospels do not agree in the names between David and Joseph. We should see the genealogies as less of an Ancestry.com map and more of a metaphorical one. Matthew insists on Jesus' Davidic descent, but Luke stresses an alternative form of kingdom, one not based on royal privilege. Indeed, throughout Luke-Acts, our author contrasts Jesus and his followers with those in dynastic succession: Herod the Great, Herod Antipas, Herod Agrippa I, Herod Agrippa II. Matthew stresses not only the connections of Jesus to David but also the connections of Jesus to other figures in Israel's Scriptures, including Solomon. Indeed, without the mention of Solomon, Matthew could not have included "the wife of Uriah" in the genealogy. Matthew also has a very special reason for identifying the father of Joseph as Jacob.

Joseph, Son of Jacob

Matthew ends the genealogy with the notice, "Jacob was the father of Joseph, the husband of Mary—of whom Jesus was born, who is called the Christ" (1:16). Biblically knowledgeable readers will connect this "Jacob was the father of Joseph" with an earlier Jacob the father of Joseph. We are again back in Genesis. We had been there already with Abraham, Isaac, and Jacob (the first Jacob in the genealogy), as well as Judah and Tamar. That original Jacob had twelve

Matthew insists on Jesus' Davidic descent, but Luke stresses an alternative form of kingdom, one not based on royal privilege. Indeed, throughout Luke-Acts, our author contrasts Jesus and his followers with those in dynastic succession.

sons, one of whom is the son of his beloved wife, Rachel (her voice is heard in Matthew's second chapter), the famous Joseph (perhaps best known now for his "amazing technicolor dreamcoat").

That first Joseph dreamed dreams, was sold by his brothers into slavery, was delivered to Egypt, survived the enticements of Potiphar's wife (we may here briefly be reminded of the hints of scandal that could have accompanied, but did not, Tamar, Rahab, Ruth, and Bathsheba), and eventually rescued not only his family but all of Egypt from famine. That first Joseph dies in Egypt, but he too returns to his home. At the Exodus, "Moses took with him Joseph's bones just as Joseph had made Israel's sons promise when he said to them, 'When God takes care of you, you must carry my bones out of here with you'" (Exodus 13:19).

Knowing the ancient story, Matthew's readers can anticipate that the second Joseph, son of Jacob, will dream dreams, take his family to Egypt to protect them, and return to the land of Israel. Since that original Joseph is the father of Ephraim, the eponymous ancestor of the main Northern tribe, we readers can even expect this second Joseph to relocate north, to Galilee. We are not disappointed.

Being a Righteous Man

Joseph and Mary are legally betrothed; although they had not yet married, both the cultural and legal expectation was that Mary would be faithful to Joseph. Then Joseph learns that his betrothed is pregnant. We readers know, because Matthew tells us, that the child is "by the Holy Spirit" (Matthew 1:18). Joseph does not know this. All he knows is that his wife-to-be is also a mother-to-be, and he is not happy about the situation.

He does not make a public spectacle of Mary, because as Matthew tells us, he is a "righteous" man (the Greek term, *dikaios*, is related to the term usually translated "justification"). That term in various

forms appears numerous times in the Gospel to set the standard for behavior. In the Sermon on the Mount, Jesus instructs, "unless your righteousness is greater than the righteousness of the legal experts and the Pharisees, you will never enter the kingdom of heaven" (5:20). He is setting the bar very high. According to the parable of the sheep and the goats, it is the "righteous" who saw Jesus in the face of the hungry and the thirsty and who responded with kindness and service. It is consequently the righteous who receive eternal life (25:37, 46). We learn at the end of Matthew's Gospel that Jesus epitomizes righteousness, although we may miss the point because of English translations. The NRSV reports that Pontius Pilate's wife sent word to him while he was sitting on the judgment seat and about to condemn Jesus, "Have nothing to do with that innocent man." The CEB is truer to the Greek translation: "Leave that *righteous* man alone" (27:19, italics added).

The righteous Joseph resolves to divorce Mary quietly (1:19): no public stink, no demands for money. This divorce procedure fits with what we know of Jewish legal practice. Because the engagement is a legal contract, it requires a divorce document for nullification.

We've already noted that a number of uninformed commentators assert that Joseph acted quietly to prevent Mary's being stoned to death on the charge of adultery. This is bad history. David and Bathsheba were clearly guilty of adultery, but they are not executed. No one in the Bible is. The rabbinic tradition does whatever it can to prevent the death penalty from ever being carried out.

It is better here to think about Joseph, the righteous man, the one who at first thought it best to annul the marriage. Perhaps he thought that Mary was in love with someone else. Since he resolves to engage the legal process quietly, likely he was concerned for her reputation. Perhaps he loved her. The Gospel reminds us of human problems and prompts us to think of human responses. I imagine that, had Joseph

gone through with the divorce, Mary and her child would have been cared for by the people of Nazareth. With all the finger-pointing and tongues wagging that today often come with unplanned pregnancies, it is good to imagine that kindness could replace contempt.

I mention this issue of stoning, both because I've read it in a number of sermons and because I experienced firsthand how wrong such an interpretation can go. Several years ago, I was doing a scholar-in-residence program for a large Protestant church. The conveners asked me if I wanted to give the sermon Sunday morning, and since it was Advent and the lectionary for the date I was to visit was about John the Baptist, I happily agreed (yes, I do preach in Christian settings, but I do not read aloud the Gospel text on which the sermon is based).

The 8:30 a.m. service in the chapel worked well, as did the 11:00 a.m. service in the main sanctuary. The third service was "alternative worship" in the gymnasium. Instead of a choir, there was a praise band; instead of a hymnal, lyrics were projected on screens, with background images of trees and beaches and oceans. Then came a liturgical dance performed by a teenager wearing a dress made from a sheet and a matching pillow case for a veil (it looked better than it sounds). Completing the steps, she announced to an older woman, in similar sheeting, "Mother, I am pregnant." The mother, horrified, screams, "You've committed adultery; you have to be stoned." The praise band took up the chant, "Stone her, stone her," and all the little kids got up and clapped and shouted, "Stone her, stone her." "Mary" then announced that with the coming of her son, no longer will people be under Jewish law, which kills, but under Christian grace, which saves.

Following such bad theology (remember Marcion), I decided to skip John the Baptist and talk about Jesus in his Jewish context. Apparently, the substitute sermon worked well because the

congregation did not resume the chant, "Stone her, stone her." One does not need to invent a negative image of Judaism in order to see the grace of the Christmas story.

All is resolved. An angel appears to Joseph in a dream (of course) and tells him that Mary's child is from the Holy Spirit and that he should marry her. The angel also announces that her son, to be named "Jesus," will "save his people from their sins" (Matthew 1:21). The name *Jesus* comes from the Hebrew root meaning "to save" (as well as the names *Hosea* and *Joshua*, as well as the invocation *Hosannah*, which means "save now" or "save, please"). Joseph, the model of righteousness, does as the angel instructs.

The Virgin Will Conceive

The angel assures Joseph that Mary's pregnancy is part of the divine plan: "Now all of this [that is, the conception] took place so that what the Lord had spoken through the prophet would be fulfilled: / *Look! A virgin will become pregnant and give birth to a son,* / *And they will call him,* Emmanuel. / (*Emmanuel* means 'God with us.')" (1:22-23). The citation is from the Greek translation of Isaiah 7:14. In the Hebrew original, Isaiah simply states, "Look, the young woman is pregnant." There is no reference to a virgin or, more accurately, to "the virgin" (we can picture Isaiah pointing to someone in the king's court), and any reader would conclude that the young woman's pregnancy was no more or less a miracle than any other pregnancy.

When the Hebrew text was translated into Greek, about two centuries before Matthew's Gospel, the Hebrew word *alma*, meaning "young woman," became *parthenos*, a term that can mean "virgin." Nashville, where I live, boasts a replica of the Parthenon, the Greek temple dedicated to Athena, the virgin goddess of wisdom. (When we first moved to Nashville, the taxi driver told us that the Nashville Parthenon is better than the one in Greece, "because ours is newer.")

The Greek translator also changed the Hebrew adjective "pregnant" to a future verb, "will conceive." Thus, the Greek reads, "The virgin will conceive."

It is not clear that the Greek translators were anticipating a miracle. First, the Greek translation of Genesis 34, the story of how Jacob's daughter Dinah has sexual relations with a local prince named Shechem, describes Dinah, after that initial encounter, as a *parthenos*, here, a young woman. More likely, Isaiah's Greek translator wanted the connotation of "virgin" in order to extend the time period before the sign takes place: the virgin will conceive, the narrator tells us, with the implication that first she will be married, then the relationship will be consummated, and then she will become pregnant.

Matthew legitimately interprets the Greek translation of Isaiah as indicating a miracle. The Jewish tradition knew of other miraculous births, and not only from the pagan cultures surrounding them. Jewish texts speak of the miraculous conceptions of Isaac, of Melchizedek, and of others. In the Jewish texts, there is no sense of the loves (and lusts) of the pagan gods; there is a sense rather of the special roles the children would play. For Matthew, the virginal conception is one more indication, along with the other fulfillment citations in the first two chapters and then throughout the Gospel, that Jesus is the fulfillment of salvation history.

By the second century CE, the followers of Jesus, knowing the Greek of Isaiah 7:14, were debating the meaning of this sign with Jews who read from the Hebrew. There is little reason to argue over who has the correct reading here. Isaiah's words will mean, and should mean, different things to different people over time. Moreover, different translations necessarily give rise to different interpretations, and translation itself is an act of interpretation.

King Uzziah, to whom Isaiah was speaking, could not have anticipated the sign would come to fulfillment seven hundred years later. That does not make Matthew's reading wrong; it rather makes

it retrospective. Jesus' followers, looking to their older Scriptures, will necessarily see new things. Such new insights should continue into the future as well, because even a fulfillment citation does not exhaust the meaning of the text being cited.

The second part of the angel's quotation actually has the greater import when it comes to understanding Matthew's Gospel: "*And they will call him,* Emmanuel. / (*Emmanuel* means 'God with us')" (1:23). For Matthew, the presence of the divine is found in Jesus. The last line of the Gospel reinforces this point, when Jesus tells his disciples, "Look, I myself will be with you every day until the end of this present age" (28:20).

Matthew's first chapter ends with the notice that when Joseph woke up, he did what the angel had commanded him to do. He married Mary. However, he had no marital relations with her until the baby was born. The last line of the chapter is, "Joseph called him Jesus" (1:25, an echo of the angel's command in 1:21). Both names, Jesus and Emmanuel, go together: this child, who will be with his followers, will save them.

But not yet, for as Matthew's next chapter reveals, Mary and Joseph and others first have to save the child.

King Herod and the Magi

Matthew's second chapter opens with the notice of the rule of "King Herod." That word *king* introduces a choice for readers: to follow "King Herod," propped up by the Roman Empire and ruling by intimidation and violence, or to follow the new king, already introduced as "son of David" and as part of David's royal lineage. The Evangelist brilliantly depicts the challenge to King Herod in the opening verse, when the Magi (which is how the text identifies them) enter Jerusalem and ask, "Where is the newborn king of the Jews?" (2:2).

One could argue that the
Magi are kings, although
Matthew never makes the point
explicitly....To the contrary,
the Magi represent both
political machinations
and pagan wisdom.

Matthew packs numerous points into this question. First, the inquiry about this newborn king is tremendously impolitic, for "King Herod" is not about to cede his authority to this child, or any child. Given that question, anyone who still thinks these questioners are "wise" might want to reconsider. They have just, albeit unknowingly, denied Herod's kingship.

Second, Matthew begins a pattern, seen throughout the Gospel, of depicting people in authority—whether Herod the Great or Pontius Pilate or the high priests—as working in opposition to the "kingdom of the heavens" that Jesus proclaims. Jesus even speaks about "those who rule the Gentiles show off their authority over them and their high-ranking officials order them around" (20:25): his model of servant-leadership, of being a servant to all, is the opposite.

One could argue that the Magi are kings, although Matthew never makes the point explicitly. Isaiah 60:3 speaks of kings coming to worship the God of Israel, and 60:6 adds that they will be "carrying gold and incense." But given Matthew's view of kings, to call the Magi "kings" would be odd. Nor would any early reader of Matthew's Gospel see the Magi as kings.

To the contrary, the Magi represent both political machinations and pagan wisdom. Several ancient sources record notices of a Magus (the singular of "Magi") who challenged the Persian king Cambyses in the fifth century BCE. The Roman historian Suetonius notes that Tiberius, the emperor at the time of Jesus and who was concerned about political challenge, banished all astrologers from Rome in 19 CE. Josephus, our first-century Jewish historian, mentions a Magus who arranged the marriage of the Roman governor Felix to Drusilla, the sister of Agrippa II (see Acts 24:24-25). The affair was scandalous. Acts also mentions not only Simon Magus, who tricks the Samaritans and then seeks to buy the power to bestow the Holy Spirit (see the marvelously camp movie *The Silver Chalice*, with Paul

Newman in his film debut and Jack Palance playing Simon Magus), but also Elymas Bar Jesus, in the employ of the Proconsul of Cyprus, who opposes Paul. Thus, when Magi appear in ancient sources, kings should get nervous. On the other hand, Persian legend speaks of Magi present at the birth of King Cyrus.

In fact, the Magi of Matthew 2 only start to get a royal designation after the Emperor Constantine, seeing the Greek letters *chi* and *rho* in the heavens, converts to Christianity. The sign of the letters becomes associated with the star of Bethlehem. The result of this connection was of political benefit: just as the Magi, seen now as kings, paid homage to Jesus by following his star, so the kings of the earth should pay homage to the emperor by following his sign.

Third, Matthew begins to move power away from Jerusalem, the Judean capital. The Gospel explains that when Herod heard of this rival king, he "was troubled, *and everyone in Jerusalem was troubled with him*" (Matthew 2:3, italics added). Jerusalem for Matthew is both the holy city and the place where Jesus will be betrayed, tortured, and killed. For Matthew, but not for Luke and John, the mission begins not in Jerusalem but from a mountaintop in Galilee. For Matthew, the center of power shifts.

Fourth, complementing this theme of the shifting of power and despite the Gospel's literary sophistication with its numerous references to earlier texts, Matthew insists that the message is not for the intellectuals (well, if we must, the academics) or for kings and high priests. The gospel is for those who become like children. Jesus prays, "I praise you, Father, Lord of heaven and earth, because you've hidden these things from the wise and intelligent and have shown them to babies" (11:25).

Matthew makes that point already in chapter 2 by noting that Herod, although "king of the Jews," does not know his own scripture. He has to call the "chief priests and the legal experts" to ask them

where the Messiah was to be born (2:4). That is how he and the Magi learn that the prophet Micah had announced to Bethlehem, "from you will come one who governs, who will shepherd my people Israel" (2:6). The king's advisors know the words, but they are unable or unwilling to recognize their import.

The king's advisors do have one advantage: they know the Scriptures of Israel. The Magi's astronomical knowledge, and with it foreign wisdom or Greek philosophy or what we today would call "science," only gets them so far; they need to understand the Torah and the Prophets to interpret this sign. For the biblical tradition, people outside of Israel may have wisdom and talent, but they need more. The only time Magi appear by name in the Greek translation of the Old Testament is in Daniel 2:10, where King Nebuchadnezzar summons Magi not only to interpret his dreams but also to describe them. They fail, and Nebuchadnezzar would have executed all of them had Daniel, knowledgeable in and faithful to the traditions of Israel, not intervened.

Finally, the verse and the rest of the chapter open up issues of religious respect. Magi are Zoroastrian priests. Several years ago, I did a radio show on the Christmas story, and I mentioned how much I like the Magi, not only because they stop to ask for directions, but also because they are delightfully comic figures. They speak the truth, even when they do not realize the import of their words. I then compared them to Larry, Moe, and Curly (if these are unfamiliar people to you, ask someone over the age of seventy). A Zoroastrian priest wrote to me to tell me that I should be respectful in treating other people's religious authorities. He was exactly right. I did not know at the time that Magi are priests today, but that was no excuse for my comment. How marvelous it is when a Zoroastrian priest tells a Jewish professor that her reading of a Christian text was unsympathetic.

Getting the details on the prediction regarding Bethlehem, Herod secretly calls the Magi and orders them to make a thorough search for the child. So much for a secret meeting, given that anyone who reads the Gospel knows about it. As Jesus states in Matthew 10:26, "nothing is hidden that won't be revealed, and nothing secret that won't be brought out into the open." That statement may be particularly true regarding political dealings. Then the king, dripping with irony that the Magi do not recognize, says, "report to me so that I too may go and honor him" (2:8). Herod has no such intention; he is interested in execution, not esteem. That danger will cast its shadow over the Magi's visit to the newborn king.

The Star of Bethlehem

According to Matthew, a star guided the Magi to Jerusalem, and then from Jerusalem to Bethlehem, where it stopped directly over Mary and Joseph's house. Let's think about this. Stars, which are giant balls of gas that fuse hydrogen into helium in a thermonuclear way (more information here is above my pay grade), do not function like GPS systems, first dropping the Magi off in Jerusalem and then rerouting to get them to the suburbs. (Bethlehem is about five miles south-southwest of Jerusalem.)

Moreover, Matthew tells us that the star "stood over the place where the child was" (2:9). If a star, as we understand stars, were to stop directly over a house, that house would be incinerated, as would the rest of the earth. Therefore, the incessant articles attempting to explain the star scientifically—planetary conjunctions such as between Jupiter and Saturn in 7 BCE, Haley's comet visible in late summer 12 BCE, supernovas, such as the one in the constellation Capricorn in 5 BCE, or between Venus and Jupiter in 2 BCE— misread Matthew. The star of Bethlehem is not about science; it is about the search for meaning.

The star of Matthew's second chapter is not a star as we understand stars. People in antiquity did not know about thermonuclear fusion or even how big stars are. In the ancient world, stars were sentient beings, gods, or the souls of the righteous or angels. The star is thus a heavenly messenger, not a science lesson.

The Gifts of the Magi

January 6, the Feast of the Epiphany, celebrates the arrival of the Magi. They arrive not at a stable (that would be Luke) or a cave (as in the *Protevangelium of James*) but at a house with a star shining above. As Matthew puts it, they followed the star "until it stood over the place where the child was. When they saw the star, they were filled with joy" (2:9-10). The verse has always sounded to me as if they rejoiced upon arrival, as children in the back seat might say, "Are we there yet?" I can picture a storyteller acting out this scene, with the Magi getting off their camels (no, Matthew does not mention camels) and stretching.

Whereas King Herod and his court know the location of this new king, it is gentile Magi, not Temple authorities or the nominal "king of the Jews," who come to the home. Matthew's point is not Jewish failures and gentile successes, for Mary and Joseph are also Jews. It is rather that some Jews and some gentiles will accept Jesus' message, as Matthew has already indicated by incorporating both Jews and gentiles into the genealogy. Others, such as the Jewish Herod and Caiaphas the High Priest and the gentile soldiers and their commander, Pontius Pilate, will not.

Not only do the Magi visit the child, but also they bring gifts, the famous gold, frankincense, and myrrh. A number of years ago, the *New Yorker Magazine* published a cartoon of Mary and Joseph sitting on the floor and opening gifts. The caption read something like, "Good, there's a receipt for the myrrh." Matthew does not tell

us whether the gifts had any symbolic value, but the absence has not stopped speculation. Irenaeus, the second-century Church Father from Lyon, proposed that the gifts had practical purposes: the gold represented Jesus' royal status; the myrrh was to anoint his corpse and so to show his humanity; the frankincense, which was burnt on altars, symbolized his divinity.

When I look for the symbolic meaning of a biblical image or statement, I look first for other places in the Bible where the image or words appear. Although chapter 2 is the only place in Matthew's Gospel where frankincense is mentioned, gold does show up elsewhere. Jesus tells his disciples that when they go out to proclaim the gospel, they are not to gather "gold or silver or copper coins" (10:9). Thus, we learn that despite the Magi's generosity, Jesus is not a king who needs gold. Later, Jesus will ask the Pharisees and scribes, "Which is greater, the gold or the temple that makes the gold holy?" (23:17); the place of worship is of greater import than the gold in one's belt. Myrrh makes a singular appearance in Matthew's Gospel, but Irenaeus was not wrong in connecting it to Jesus' corpse. Irenaeus was likely thinking of John 19:39, which tells us that Nicodemus, when he came to help Joseph of Arimathea entomb Jesus' body, brought "a mixture of myrrh and aloe, nearly seventy-five pounds in all." That's a lot of myrrh. Finally, the Scriptures of Israel consistently associate frankincense with offerings in the Temple. When it came to the gifts, Irenaeus knew his scripture!

Interpretation of the gifts is part of the ongoing story, as is the upgrading of the Magi from astrologers to kings. The stories continue. The idea that there were three Magi comes from the three gifts. There may have been seven Magi, or ten, or more. As church patronage developed, wealthy donors would arrange to have themselves and their family members depicted as Magi who had come to worship the Christ Child. They are dressed to impress. The eventual depiction of

Irenaeus, the second-century Church Father from Lyon, proposed that the gifts had practical purposes: the gold represented Jesus' royal status; the myrrh was to anoint his corpse and so to show his humanity; the frankincense, which was burnt on altars, symbolized his divinity.

the Magi as three kings, Caspar, Melchior, and Balthasar, likely comes from Psalm 72:10-11, which reads, "Let the kings of Tarshish and the islands bring tribute; / let the kings of Sheba and Seba present gifts. / Let all the kings bow down before him; / let all the nations serve him." The Psalm is labeled "of Solomon," and Jesus is, in Matthew's Gospel (but not Luke's), a direct descendant of Solomon. The kings came to represent the children of Noah, Ham, Shem, and Japheth, or Africa, Asia, and Europe. In some early art, their depiction is almost exactly the same as the depiction of the three youths in the fiery furnace of Daniel 3 (today, probably best known as Rack, Shack, and Benny from *Veggie Tales*). By the year 490, the Byzantine emperor Zeno claimed to have found the relics of the three kings; the relics then make their way from Constantinople to Milan to Cologne (the final trip in 1164 thanks to Barbarossa), and that's where they can be visited today, by wise men, or tourists. The venerable Bede, an eighth-century British monk who identifies the Magi by name, may have been the first who called them "wise men"; Bede, a wise man, commended their search for truth but not their astrological approach.

Mary and Joseph do not say anything to the Magi, or the Magi to them. The import for Matthew is their presence, indicating the universal rule of this new child, the yielding of all ancient wisdom to him, and the honor he receives from the equivalent of ancient science. The scene ends with the notice that the Magi, like Joseph and Pilate's wife, received dreams of warning. Advised against returning to Herod (they did not realize that this king had plans other than paying homage to Jesus), "they went back to their own country by another route" (Matthew 2:12). They travel out of the text and into legend.

I do wonder if Matthew is hinting at something more. The Greek for "route" is *hodos* (whence the term *odometer*). According to the

Book of Acts, people who gathered in the name of Jesus were not called "Christian"; the term is in fact very rare in New Testament texts. They were called "followers of the way" (*hodos*). Thus, the Magi, like the shepherds in Luke, become early evangelists. Neither group has the full story, but they are on the way.

A New Moses

We do not know how long it took before Herod realized that the Magi had duped him: two weeks, two months? One can walk from Bethlehem to Jerusalem in a day. However long, Herod was not going to risk his rule.

It is in this period of danger that an angel appears to Joseph in a dream; this time the command is another disruption: "Get up," the angel orders. "Take the child and his mother and escape to Egypt. Stay there until I tell you," for Herod seeks the child's life (2:13). Obedient as before, the righteous Joseph takes the child and his mother by night and flees to Egypt (2:14). This is the first account of refugees in the New Testament. Attentive readers immediately note what Matthew is doing; Matthew is connecting Jesus to both the story of Israel and, more particularly, to the story of Moses.

The Book of Exodus recounts how Pharaoh planned to kill all of Israel's sons as soon as they were born. Moses escapes the slaughter when his mother places him in an ark and floats this ark down the Nile. Now Jesus will survive, with the help of his parents, while other children will lose their lives. The parallels to Moses continue. Like Moses, Jesus will leave Egypt and move to Israel, but while Moses dies outside the land, Jesus lives in it. In Matthew's next chapter, Jesus, like Moses, enters water and experiences a life-changing event, as the parting of the Red Sea finds a new meaning in Jesus' baptism. According to Matthew 4, Jesus goes into the wilderness for forty days, where he faces temptation and emerges triumphant;

he recollects the forty years in the wilderness, where ancient Israel succumbed to temptation and worshiped a golden calf (this was not one of Israel's better moments). Finally, Jesus gathers his disciples, ascends a mountain, and delivers instruction on how to live. The Sermon on the Mount, Matthew 5–7 (that sermon deserves a study of its own), confirms that Jesus is a new Moses, who received the Torah on Mount Sinai. Jesus, in the footsteps of Moses, does not abolish the Torah (God forbid); to the contrary he states, "Don't even begin to think that I have come to do away with the Law and the Prophets. I haven't come to do away with them but to fulfill them" (5:17). Readers of the first two chapters, which are full of quotations and allusions to the Torah and Prophets, already know this.

Jesus, Mary, and Joseph remain in Egypt until Herod dies. Matthew tells us that the flight to Egypt and the eventual return to the land of Israel fulfills Hosea 11:1: "out of Egypt I called my son." Now, Matthew tells us, Jesus is repeating Israel's story and in doing so is giving it new meaning.

Slaughter, Weeping, and Resurrection

While the family remains safely in Egypt, Herod takes action. His offense (in all soundings of the term) is to send his soldiers to Bethlehem and kill all the children in the city and the region around it, who are two years old and younger. There is a difference between a newborn and a toddler, but the soldiers do not take the time to look. Nor do they distinguish boys from girls.

No ancient sources other than Matthew record the "Slaughter of the Innocents," and no one mentions it again even in Matthew's Gospel. For me, the issue is less one of the historians' endless debate about "did this happen?" or "did Matthew invent the scene to increase the connection between Jesus and Moses?" For me, the greater import is what the story suggests about despair and what comes after.

As the parents cry out in anguish, Matthew tells us that they are not alone and that God is aware of their suffering. This tragedy, like all tragedies, is a consequence of free will. Matthew writes, "This fulfilled the word spoken through Jeremiah the prophet, *A voice was heard in Ramah.*" The voice was that of Rachel, the matriarch who dies giving birth to Jacob's youngest son, Benjamin, and who is buried on the roadside. Rachel is *"weeping for her children, and she did not want to be comforted, because they were no more"* (Matthew 2:17-18). In the original context, Jeremiah envisioned Rachel watching the inhabitants of Jerusalem being taken into Babylonian exile, their Temple burned to the ground, their city in ruins.

There is another page to the story. This fulfillment citation is from Jeremiah 31, the famous chapter that also speaks of the new covenant (Jeremiah 31:31) that God will make, when God will forgive the sins of Israel (Jeremiah 31:34). To understand what Matthew is doing, we need to know the verse that comes after Rachel's lament. God reassures the mourning mother, "Keep your voice from crying and your eyes from weeping. . . . There's hope for your future. . . . Your children will return home!" (Jeremiah 31:16-17). The world is hopeless for parents whose children have died. Matthew recognizes the grief; it does not stop. The story of these children, and their murder, must be preserved. For Jeremiah, Rachel's prayer was for the return from exile, and that prayer was answered when Cyrus of Persia conquered Babylon and told the captives "the LORD, the God of heaven . . . has instructed me to build a temple for him at Jerusalem in Judah. Whoever among you belong to God's people, let them go up, and may the LORD their God be with them!" (2 Chronicles 36:23). This message of return is the last line in the Tanakh, as 2 Chronicles is the last book of the Hebrew Bible that is read by Jews in the synagogue.

For Matthew, there is another answer to Rachel's weeping, another return. For Matthew, the prayer is answered in the ongoing

presence of Jesus and, finally, in the resurrection of the dead and the Last Judgment.

Today we speak of survivors' guilt. We live when a tragedy such as an accident, a war, or a fire takes the life of others. For many of these survivors, a new dedication to life can arise: a concern to save others and so make the life spared a life that truly counts. It is common to say that "God spared someone," but that does not help, since it suggests that God cared less about the others. It is also common to hear, "God wanted these precious ones to come to heaven now," but that doesn't help either; it suggests that God cares less about those who still live. The ways of God in such circumstances are unknown. Matthew tells us that when tragedy happens, God is "with us" (Emmanuel). In the Jewish tradition, one greets people in mourning by saying, "May their memory be for a blessing." How is that done? By acting in their name with kindness and compassion, we honor their memory.

Return and New Beginning

Herod's plans did not succeed. When he dies, again an angel makes a dream appearance and tells Joseph to take the child and his mother from Egypt and return to the land of Israel. Joseph complies, but realizing that Herod's son Archelaus was ruling Judea and so Bethlehem, he fears returning home. Matthew states, "having been warned"—and we can hear the congregation respond, "in a dream"—Joseph relocates to Galilee and settles in Nazareth. This move, too, was according to plan, for it fulfilled "what was spoken through the prophets," namely, "He will be called a Nazarene" (Matthew 2:22-23).

There is no such quotation. Some readers, made nervous by this fact, suggest that it must have dropped out of every copy of the Hebrew Bible that we have. Unlikely. Still others propose that Matthew is alluding to Nazirites, individuals who take vows of

holiness (see Numbers 6). Still others, having a stronger claim, find a relation to Isaiah 11:1-2, where the ancient prophet describes the ideal king: "A shoot will grow up from the stump of Jesse; / a branch [*netzer*, which sounds somewhat like *Nazorean*] will sprout from his roots. / The LORD's spirit will rest upon him, / a spirit of wisdom and understanding, / a spirit of planning and strength, / a spirit of knowledge and fear of the LORD." Could be.

I like to think that Matthew is being both playful and predictive. You can search all you want, says the Evangelist, and you will not find this text in the Scriptures of Israel. But there is still prophecy, Matthew knows. There are prophets in Corinth and Rome, there are Philip's four prophetic daughters in Caesarea (Acts 21:9). It is these prophets who will speak of Jesus of Nazareth. Prophets today still do.

As we read through the rest of Matthew's Gospel, the major and minor chords of the first two chapters will continue to provide the background music: of righteousness and of the presence of the divine with us, of faithful women and the coming of some gentiles to worship the God of Israel, of reversals of fortune, where the poor and hungry will be filled and the rich will learn to share, of the challenge of kingship, of danger, of people displaced. Set at a particular time and in particular places, the first two chapters of Matthew continue to hold meaning, because the stories that they tell are also our stories.

NOTE

1. "Here I Am, Lord," words by Dan Schutte, 1981, *The United Methodist Hymnal* (Nashville, TN: The United Methodist Publishing House, 1989), 593.